# Getting a Job in Australia

*Othe related titles published by How To Books*

**Living & Working in Australia**
*All you need to know for starting a new life 'down under'*

**Getting into Australia**
*The complete immigration guide to gaining your visa*

**Getting a Job Abroad**
*The handbook for the international jobseeker*

**Living & Working in New Zealand**
*How to build a new life in New Zealand*

**Retire Abroad**
*Your complete guide to a new life in the sun*

**howto**books

Please send for a free copy of the latest catalogue to:
How To Books
3 Newtec Place, Magdalen Road,
Oxford OX4 1RE, United Kingdom
email: info@howtobooks.co.uk
www.howtobooks.co.uk

# Getting a Job in Australia

*A step-by-step guide to finding work Down Under*

**NICK VANDOME**

*5th edition*

**howto**books

*Acknowledgement*
Commonwealth data included in this publication is copyright and reproduced by permission. Apart from any use as permitted under the *Copyright Act 1968*, no part may be reproduced by any process without prior written permission from the Australian Government Publishing Service. Requests and inquiries concerning reproduction and rights should be directed to the Manager, Commonwealth Information Services, Australian Government Publishing Service, GPO Box 84, Canberra, ACT 2610.

Published by How To Books Ltd,
3 Newtec Place, Magdalen Road,
Oxford OX4 1RE, United Kingdom.
Tel: (01865) 793806. Fax: (01865) 248780.
email: info@howtobooks.co.uk
www.howtobooks.co.uk

First edition 1992
Second edition 1995
Third edition 1997
Fourth edition 2000
Reprinted 2001
Fifth edition 2004

British Library Cataloguing in Publication Data
A catalogue record for this book is available from
the British Library.

Produced for How To Books by Deer Park Productions, Tavistock
Typeset by Anneset, Weston-super-Mare, N Somerset
Cover design by Baseline Arts Ltd, Oxford
Printed and bound by Cromwell Press, Trowbridge, Wiltshire.

NOTE: The material contained in this book is set out in good faith for general guidance and no liability can be accepted for loss or expense incurred as a result of relying in particular circumstances on statements made in the book. Laws and regulations are complex and liable to change, and readers should check the current position with the relevant authorities before making personal arrangements.

# Contents

# List of Illustrations

# Preface

Australia has attracted the interest of vast numbers of people world-wide in the last fifty years: since the end of World War Two over five million migrants have settled there. The British, as much as any other nation, are fascinated with Australia and all things Australian. At the beginning of the 1990s this interest remained undiminished, despite an economic recession in Australia that led to higher unemployment and calls for curbs on migration.

However, the new millennium has seen a continuation of the economic revival that began in the mid-1990s. Unemployment is heading to under 6%, inflation is low and growth is predicted at a healthy 5% for at least the next couple of years. This has led the Australian Government to ease the immigration quotas and allow more people into the country, particularly skilled workers.

The last few years have also seen the federal government firmly embracing new technology, with the result that there is now an extensive range of information on the Web. This edition of Getting a Job in Australia reflects this and, where possible, Web addresses have been included for both government and private organisations. A full list of Web address is given at the end of the book.

Despite the upturn in the Australian economy and the job market, the situation is still a far cry from the halcyon days of the 1960s. Prospective migrants and workers should not be lulled into a false sense of optimism. There are jobs available, but what is needed when looking for a job is careful thought and a certain amount of research. This book does not promise to land you a top post with a multi-national company, but it will arm you with all the relevant information that you need to tackle the job scene in Australia.

I am indebted to various people who helped me in gathering much of the factual information for the new editions of this book. This includes a number of unnamed officials in both Australia and Britain. If migrants and job hunters enjoy the same excellent service then they will be well on their way to a successful life in Australia.

I hope this book will be of some use to people heading off to forge a living Down Under. If readers notice any errors or omissions, please contact the author c/o How To Books.

*Nick Vandome*

# 1

## Economic Overview

### ECONOMIC ROOTS

The first 'employees' of Australia were the 800 convicts who sailed with the First Fleet which arrived in Australia on 26th January 1788. Although conditions were harsh the new settlers were determined to forge as prosperous a life as possible in their new home. Those who were released from the convict settlements, or who went to Australia as willing settlers, soon found that it was a land rich in natural resources.

Agriculture was the first boom industry and by 1819 a Scotsman named Captain John Macarthur had built up a flock of over 6,000 merino sheep. This proved to be only the beginning for the Australian sheep population and by 1850 there were over 18 million sheep of various varieties, providing over half the wool imported by England.

The expansion of the sheep population led to increased demands on the land, which in turn spawned a contingent of pioneers who traversed the massive spaces of this vast land. One of the results of their exploits was the discovery of Australia's enormous mineral wealth. In the 1850s large gold finds were made in New South Wales and Victoria, which brought a stampede of prospectors from Europe, America and China. Inevitably this led to the discovery of other minerals: between 1889 and 1920 more than 170 million ounces of silver were mined at Broken Hill in New South Wales. This was supplemented by equally impressive amounts of gold, lead and zinc. The company which first exploited this, Broken Hill Proprietary Limited (BHP) is now the largest corporation in Australia.

Based partly on their economic wealth, Australians gradually began to have a growing sense of nationhood. On 1st January 1901 the Commonwealth of Australia came into being.

The Australian economy has changed dramatically over the last fifty years, as it has reacted to events including World War Two, the post-war boom, the oil crisis of the 1970s and the world-wide recession of the 1980s. The main result of these changes is that the economy has switched from a heavy reliance on primary production to a greater dependence on production in the services (tertiary) sector.

Whatever else World War Two did for Australia it had a profound effect on the economy. Manufacturing developed much faster than it would have under normal circumstances and this, coupled with an expansive immigration programme at the end of the war, ensured that the 1950s and 1960s were a boom period in Australia. There was a rapid expansion in secondary industry and large-scale investment in export-orientated mining and energy projects. Australia became regarded as an extremely desirable place to live; a country with a strong economy and a high standard of living. It more than justified its tag of the 'Lucky Country'.

Australia, and the rest of the world, was brought down to earth with a bump in the 1970s due to the OPEC oil crisis. As oil prices soared the years of low inflation and low unemployment were turned on their heads as both figures began to rise alarmingly. This continued for most of the 1970s and in the early 1980s there was an investment boom as companies strove to develop Australia's massive reserves of natural resources. However, the expected 'resources boom' was not fulfilled and in 1982/83 the Australian economy experienced a biting recession. Two years later the collapse in commodity prices harmed the economy still further — the subsequent balance of payments crisis led to stringent policy measures to try and redress the situation. These consisted of carefully developed prices-and-incomes policies and structural reforms.

In 1987 the Australian economy took a further buffeting with the world-wide stock market crash of 'Black October'. Hundreds of companies and financial institutions went to the wall and confidence in the economy was severely dented. At the same time there was a sharp downturn in the agricultural industry — traditionally one of Australia's strongest areas. Farms' incomes fell by up to fifty per cent and the economy is now just beginning to recover after the recession of the late 1980s and early 1990s.

## GENERAL ECONOMIC CONDITIONS

One of the strongest areas of the Australian economy is its natural resources and extractive industries: mineral products account for more than one third of all exports. Australia is one of the world's largest coal exporters and also a major supplier of iron ore, gold, bauxite and alumina. On a rural front Australia is still the largest producer of wool and also a major supplier of wheat, meat and sugar.

In the last fifteen years Australians have recognised the need to keep a close link between wages and taxation. This was typified in 1983 when the **Prices and Incomes Accord** came into being. This was an agreement between the Federal Government and the powerful Australian Council of Trade Unions which set out to modify wage increases in return for various tax trade-offs which resulted in increases in disposable income. This policy still forms the basis for most wage negotiations.

In 1984 the **Prices Surveillance Authority** was established as part of the prices and incomes policy. It is intended to supplement the Prices and Incomes Accord by encouraging prices restraint in response to wage restraint.

In 1989 the **Industries Commission** was formed to advise the Australian Government on matters of structural change within the economy. The Government's intention was to optimise the use of the country's natural resources and expand its productive potential. This has been a success and has led to the increased competitiveness of Australian manufacturers and services in world markets.

Most exchange controls were abolished in 1983, when the Australian dollar was floated. After a sharp initial fall the $A has remained relatively stable — usually between $A2-2.50 to the pound.

The Federal Budget is presented every August. Federal Government spending accounts for approximately a quarter of Australia's Gross Domestic Product, while state, territorial and local government spending accounts for a further fifth. About three-quarters of total public-sector revenue is raised by the Federal Government and a quarter of expenditure goes on payments to state, territorial and local governments. Individual states and territories are responsible for running services such as education, health, housing and transport but they do receive federal funding for this.

Although in theory individual states and territories can levy their own taxes (except customs and excise duties) they rarely do and for over fifty years the Federal Government has been solely responsible for income taxes on companies and individuals. Revenue comes from payroll taxes, taxes on property, financial transactions, motor-vehicle tax and franchise taxes. Australia has agreements with a number of countries to ensure that they avoid double taxation.

The Australian banking system comprises the central bank (the Reserve Bank of Australia) and 35 banks or banking groups which operate under its supervision. There are also approximately 120 money-market corporations.

Fig. 1. Map of Australia

## THE CURRENT SITUATION

It is impossible to discuss the recent Australian economy without mentioning the R-word — recession ravaged the Australian economy at the end of the 1980s and the beginning of the 1990s. One of the main victims of the recession was Bob Hawke who was ousted from power in January 1992 by his former Treasurer, Paul Keating. Australians were becoming increasingly frustrated with high unemployment and high interest rates and it was thought that it was time for a change in an attempt to bring an end to one of the worst recessions in recent years. Mr Hawke was the only Prime Minister in Australian history to have won four consecutive elections and he was the country's second longest serving premier, having held the post for eight years, nine months and eight days.

Paul Keating remained in power until 1996 when the Liberal party, led by John Howard, ousted him following his perceived failure to deliver the economic reforms that had been promised. In March 1996 John Howard was elected Prime Minister of a Liberal Party coalition government, a position that was consolidated in election in February 2000. Since then the Australian economy has remained robust, despite a weak world economy and a serious drought in 2002/03. It is predicted that the economy will continue to grow through 2004, but at a slightly slower pace than in recent years. Solid employment growth should see the unemployment rate remain around current levels of 6% and inflation is forecast to decline to around the middle of the 2–3 percent target band. The biggest threat to Australian economic growth is deterioration in the world economy. Despite the drought, the Australian economy was one of the developed world's top-performing economies in 2003.

On the immigration front, things are also looking up. Following a decline in immigration numbers in 1997–98 and 1998–1999, the recent figures show that the numbers are now increasing. In 1999–2000 there were 70,000 immigration places in total into Australia and in 2000–2001 this increased to 76,000. This can only be good news for people seeking employment, particularly as nearly half of this number will be in the skilled migration category. Announcing the 2001–2000 figures Philip Ruddock, the then Minister for Immigration and Multicultural Affairs, announced that there would be an additional 5,000 places for a new Skill Stream category: "The further shift in the balance of the Program towards the Skill Stream will deliver additional economic, budgetary and employment benefits, particularly given the skill shortages that have emerged in the Australian economy," The Minister said that a 5,000 increase in the Skill Stream has become possible because of the success of the new points test in attracting young migrants with strong English language skills and qualifications in high demand occupations such as IT and accounting.

All in all the tide seems to have turned following a dip in both the economy and immigration numbers and the future looks brighter than ever for those who want to forge a new beginning in the Lucky Country.

# 2

# Entry Requirements

## GENERAL

The first thing to consider when looking for a job in Australia is, obviously, getting into the country. For people of working age (men under 65 and women under 60) this can be done through four categories:

1.  Skilled Independent Migration.
2.  Employer Nomination Scheme.
3.  Business Migration.
4.  Holiday Working Visa.

The first of these categories operate on a **points system** and applicants will have to achieve a certain score before they are considered. This is to show that they will be able to join the work force quickly and support themselves without government help.

Since the beginning of 1992 the Australian Government has reintroduced the **pool system** for people wishing to migrate to Australia. The pool system, first introduced in 1989 to give the Government flexible management of their migration policy, gives potential migrants more than one chance to emigrate. Once they achieve the entrance mark to join the pool they are either accepted for emigration because they have enough points to reach the priority pass mark, or if they do not reach this mark, they can remain in the pool and have their points total assessed against any new pass marks which will allow them to emigrate. Further information on emigration can be found at these Web sites: www.australia.org.uk and www.fed.gov.au

**SKILLED INDEPENDENT MIGRATION**

The current score for skilled independent migration, at the time of writing, to join the pool system is 105. The score for a priority pass mark is 110. In addition to categories for skills, age and language skills there are also categories for areas such as Australian qualifications and bonus points.

### Points for Skill:

The occupation you nominate must be on the Skilled Occupations List current at the time you apply, and should be one which fits your skills and qualifications. You receive the points allocated for your nominated occupation as long as the relevant assessment authority for your nominated skilled occupation determines that your skills are suitable.

- For most occupations where training is specific to the occupation – 60 points.
- For more general professional occupations – 50 points.
- For other general skilled occupations – 40 points.

### Points for Age:

- 18 to 29 years (at time of application) – 30 points.
- 30 to 34 years – 25 points.
- 35 to 39 years – 20 points.
- 40 to 44 years – 15 points.

### Points for English Language Ability:

- Vocational English (a reasonable command of English, coping with overall meaning in most situations) – 15 points.
- Competent English – 20 points.

### Points for Specific Work Experience:

- If your nominated occupation is worth 60 points under Skill, and you have worked in your nominated occupation, or a closely related occupation, for at least 3 of the 4 years before you apply – 10 points.
- If your nominated occupation is worth 40, 50 or 60 points under Skill, and you have worked in skilled employment (any occupation

on the Skilled Occupations List) for at least 3 of the 4 years before you apply – 5 points.

### Points for Occupation in Demand/Job Offer:

A number of occupations have been identified as being in demand in Australia – the list is called the Migration Occupations in Demand List (MODL). You receive points if your nominated occupation is on the MODL which is current at the time your application is assessed.

- For occupation in demand, but no job offer – 5 points.
- For occupation in demand, with job offer – 10 points.

### Points for Australian Qualifications

Applicants with Australian qualifications have a greater chance of employment in Australia. You may receive points if you have completed an Australian qualification from an Australian educational institutional, studying for at least 12 months full-time (one academic year) in Australia. Your qualifications must be an Australian post-secondary degree (or higher qualification), diploma, advanced diploma or trade qualification.

- For an Australian qualification – 5 points.

### Points for Spouse Skills:

You may receive points if your spouse is also able to satisfy the basic requirements of age, English language ability, qualifications, nominated occupation and recent work experience and has obtained a suitable skill assessment from the relevant assessing authority for their nominated occupation.

- Points for Spouse skills – 5 points.

### Bonus Points:

You may receive points for **any one** of the following:
Capital investment in Australia (a minimum of $100 000),

Australian work experience (you must have legally worked in Australia in a specific occupation for at least six months in the four years before you apply),

Fluency in one of Australia's Community Languages (other than English).

● Bonus points – 5 points.

## Only for Skilled – Australian Sponsored Applicants
## Points for Relationship

You may receive points if you or your spouse have a relative who is an Australian citizen or permanent resident, and is willing to sponsor you. You or your spouse must be related to the sponsor as either a non-dependent child, a parent, a brother or sister, or a niece or nephew.

● Points for relationship – 15 points.

## EMPLOYER NOMINATION SCHEME

The Employer Nomination Scheme (ENS) allows Australian Employers to fill certain 'highly skilled positions' with non-Australian citizens or residents. This can be done on a permanent or a temporary basis.

There are two stages in the ENS process:

● Nomination by the employer.
● Nominee's application for a visa.

## Employer Nomination

The start of the process begins when the employer submits a completed form with all of the necessary documentation. The employer must be able to demonstrate that:

● They need a paid employee, the business is located in Australia and that they are the employer.
● The vacancy requires the appointment of a 'highly skilled person'. This usually means a person who has completed 3 years formal training, or equivalent experience, usually of 5 years.
● If applicable, the employee is eligible for any mandatory licensing, registration or professional body membership.
● The position is a full-time, fixed-term appointment of at least 3 years, which does not exclude the possibility of renewal.

- The employer has a satisfactory training record.
- The employer must be able to show that the position cannot be filled from the Australian labour market.
- The terms and conditions of employment must be in accordance with the standards for working conditions provided under Australian industrial laws.

### Nominee's application for a visa

Once they have been nominated the nominee must lodge a visa application and pay any relevant application charges. The visa application will be assessed against the following:

- That the nominee has the relevant skills.
- That the nominee meets the definition of a 'highly skilled person'.
- That the nominee is able to meet any mandatory licensing, registration or professional body membership requirements.
- That the employment is still available.
- That the nominee is less than 45 years of age.
- That the nominee has vocational English language ability.
- That the nominee, and all other family members, meet mandatory health and character requirements.

### FEES

There are considerable fees involved for people intending to emigrate. Fees for full migration are now £505 and £5 for the initial **Application for Migration** kit.

### BUSINESS SKILLS MIGRATION

In February 1992 the Australian Government introduced new rules and regulations governing business migration. The new category, **Independent— Business Skills** places greater emphasis on the skills of potential business migrants rather than the previous method of judging them solely on how much money they can take with them. They will also have to pass a similar points test to other migrant categories.

Introducing the new scheme, the then Minister for Immigration, Local Government and Ethnic Affairs, commented, 'Applicants under the new category will need to prove that they have attained a certain level of business experience and success, according to specific criteria.

They must also pass a points test which will grade them according to the size of turnover of their business, their age, English language ability, and possession of capital available for transfer.

'There will be extra points if their main business background is in a field from which Australia may get particular benefit — the manufacturing sector, trade services or in the development and use of innovative technology.'

In 1995 Business Migration was simplified and expanded to allow a wider range of skilled business people to migrate to Australia.

The Business Skills visa class of Australia's Migration Program encourages successful business people to settle permanently in Australia and develop businesses. Successive governments have re-affirmed a commitment to selecting high quality business migrants, in recognition of the benefits they contribute to Australia's increasingly global economy.

It is intended that business migrants should benefit Australia by:

* developing international markets;
* transferring capital and making investments;
* creating or maintaining employment;
* exporting Australian goods and services;
* introducing and using new or improved technology;
* substituting Australian-made products for goods that would otherwise be imported;
* adding to commercial activity and competitiveness within sectors of the Australian economy.

## Who can apply

Business owners, senior executives and investors are eligible to apply for a Business Skills visa. Business people may make an application for most Business Skills visas overseas or in Australia.

Business owners are required to demonstrate that they have had a successful business career overall and that for two of the four fiscal years preceding their application they have:

* had net assets in business of not less than AU$200 000;
* been involved in and responsible for the overall management of a business in which they have at least ten per cent ownership.

As well as meeting these requirements, business owners must pass a points test which assesses factors such as turnover, annual labour costs, total business assets, age, language ability and net personal assets.

Senior executives must demonstrate that they have had a successful business career and:

● for two of the four years preceding their application they have been employed in the top three levels of management of a business which has an annual turnover of not less than AU$50 million;

● pass a points test which assesses factors such as age, English language ability and net personal assets.

Investment-linked applicants must demonstrate a history of successful ownership and management in business and/or investment activities. In addition, applicants must:

● make an investment into a State or Territory government security of between AU$750 000 and AU$2 million, for a period of three years;

● demonstrate that they have assets worth at least 50 per cent more than their proposed investment;

● pass a points test which assesses age and English language ability.

### What must Business Migrants do after they Arrive in Australia?

Once business migrants arrive in Australia it is expected that they will:

● establish a new business;

● become an owner or part-owner of an existing business in Australia with a significant level of ownership;

● actively participate in the management of the business;

● having established a successful business as a temporary resident, remain in Australia permanently to continue that business.

The progress of business migrants is monitored after their arrival in Australia. Where no significant steps have been taken towards engaging in business within the first three years of arrival, the Minister for Immigration and Multicultural Affairs has the power to cancel the right to Australian residence of the business person and his/her family. More than seventy six visas were cancelled in 1998–99.

The fee for applicants under the Business Skills category is £1,270.

## HOLIDAY WORKING VISAS

These are available to single people, or childless couples, between the ages of 18 and 30.

The main idea behind the Holiday Working Visa is to provide young people with a chance to see Australia and supplement their travels with periods of casual employment. There are nine main conditions which applicants must fulfil:

### Conditions

1. The prime purpose of the visit is a temporary stay in Australia and permanent settlement is not intended.

2. Employment is incidental to the holiday and is to be used as a supplement to the money you bring with you.

3. Employment in Australia must not be pre-arranged except on a private basis and on the applicant's own initiative.

4. There must be a reasonable prospect of the applicant obtaining temporary employment to supplement holiday funds.

5. Applicants must show that they have reasonable funds to support themselves for some of their time in Australia, and return airfare. This is approximately £2,500 for one year.

6. Applicants must meet normal character requirements, and health standards where necessary.

7. Full-time employment should not be undertaken for more than three months with one employer.

8. Applicants must leave Australia after their Holiday Working Visa has expired.

9. The maximum length of stay is twelve months.

### Applications

Applications can be sent to any Australian Consulate in Britain and with them you will need to include:

● Three recent **passport sized photographs** of yourself, which should be signed on the back.

- **Evidence of funds** for the duration of your stay plus your return airfare. If you do not think you have enough money at the time of application it is a good idea to borrow some money, pay it into a bank or building society account, obtain a statement and then repay the money. However, it is unwise to arrive in Australia without sufficient funds. Immigration officers may not investigate your financial situation when you arrive in the country but if they do they will want to see that you have access to a substantial sum of money.

- A **valid passport**. This should be valid for at least three months *after* your proposed departure date from Australia. If your passport does not comply with this it will be necessary to get a new one.

- A stamped self-addressed envelope for the return of your passport.

You should not apply for a Working Holiday Visa more than four weeks before your proposed departure date. Application forms should be filled in carefully as incomplete ones will be returned unprocessed. It is not advisable to telephone to see how your application is progressing. This will only irritate Consulate staff and it will not hasten the arrival of your visa. People holding UK, Greek, Italian, Spanish, Irish, Canadian, Dutch or Japanese passports are all eligible to apply for Holiday Working Visas.

There is a processing fee of A\$165 for each Holiday Working Visa. This can be paid by cheque to 'Commonwealth of Australia'.

## APPLICATION POINTS

All types of visas should be sent to:

- Australian High Commission, Australia House, Strand, London WC2B 4LA. Tel: 0171 836 7123. Web site: www.australia.org.uk

- The High Commission in London is now the only place where visas can be obtained in the UK.

# 3

## Employment Law and Conditions

### PAY

The main piece of legislation governing wages in Australia is the 1983 Accord, an agreement reached by the Federal Government and the Australian Council of Trade Unions. Its aim is for the unions to cooperate with the Government's employment and anti-inflation policies; in return the Government seeks to help the unions maintain their members' living standards and eventually improve them if possible. It is an agreement that has worked well over the years and the current economic climate is maintaining this.

### 'Award rates'
Australia is a highly unionised country and because of this most wage rates are set at a minimum level. Federal and state tribunals set rates of pay for various jobs and professions and employers are then obliged to meet these 'award' rates. Seven out of eight Australian workers have their pay agreed by awards, determinations or industrial agreements. However, these figures are only a minimum recommendation and many employers pay well over the award rate.

Awards do not only cover basic rates of pay, they also deal with overtime payments and **penalty rates** — these are higher rates paid for weekend work, shift work or hours which extend past your normal hours of employment.

The award system has a number of advantages for workers. Firstly, they know what they will be paid when they apply for a job and in industries such as the retail trade it ensures that everyone is paid a reasonable wage. Secondly, the payment of penalty rates means that workers can increase their wage simply by working at the weekend, without having to work overtime. Because of this, weekend and evening work is eagerly sought by people in trades such as hospitality, whereas in Britain they would be paid at the same rates regardless of the time or the day of the week.

17

## Average wages

According to figures released in 2003 the average nationwide wage for people in full time employment was $A959, including overtime payments, although there can be big differences from state to state. New South Wales and Australian Capital Territory attract the highest wages while the lowest tend to be in Queensland and South Australia.

## HOLIDAYS

The usual holiday entitlement is four to six weeks of paid leave depending on the job and the award to which it relates. But being the fun-loving people that Australians are they do not believe that they should have to scrape by with their basic wage while they are enjoying themselves on their 'hols', so they have introduced a wonderful idea called **leave loading**. This is an exceptionally agreeable scheme whereby workers are paid an extra 17.5 per cent of their full wage while they are on holiday. All full-time employees are entitled to this bonus which some people would call a luxury but which the workers will tell you is an absolute necessity. Some firms offer a form of sabbatical leave after ten years service with a firm.

There are also national holidays on:

1st January
27th January
Easter Friday
Easter Sunday
Easter Monday
25th April
1st May (except Queensland and Northern Territory)
4th May (Northern Territory only)
8th June (except Western Australia)
25th December
26th December (except South Australia)
28th December (South Australia only).

Individual states also have their own bank holidays.

## WORKING HOURS

The standard working week is approximately 37 hours but the average hours worked within the workforce vary from 32 hours to 52.5 hours.

Hours worked above the standard working week will be paid at overtime rates of either time-and-a-half or double-time, depending on the award for that profession.

Some workers, particularly in the public sector, operate on a flexi-time system. This allows them to work a set number of hours in a four week period but within that framework it is largely up to them as to how they make up the hours. There is usually about four hours a day (core time) during which the employee must be at work but other than that they are free to come and go at times which best suit them. Additional days off can also be taken if enough flexi-time has been built up.

## TRADE UNIONS

Australia is one of the most highly unionised countries in the world and nearly half of the working population are members of unions. Trade unions have been active in Australia since the middle of the 19th century and they have fought forcefully over the years to improve working conditions and pay. There are approximately 160 unions in the country, a number which has been considerably reduced by amalgamations, and most of which are affiliated to the central organisation, the **Australian Council of Trade Unions** (ACTU), which has a total membership of around 2.5 million members.

Australia's industrial relations system remains robust but has been overhauled significantly in recent years. Since March 1994 the Industrial Relations Reform Act 1993 has been in force and this has placed greater emphasis on workplace bargaining and given increased flexibility to employers.

It was the ACTU which was responsible for forging the 1983 Accord and the national awards on pay and conditions. Every year there is a great show of negotiation between the Government and the ACTU but invariably both parties are relatively pleased with the outcome.

### Trade disputes

Industrial disputes are dealt with by state courts and tribunals, as are claims for wages and conditions. If the matters cannot be settled in this way then the matter is taken to the **Conciliation and Arbitration Commission**. This is the highest authority in the industrial set-up and is responsible for settling disputes which cannot be dealt with at a state level. Its most common duty is to arbitrate on wage claims, paying particular attention to the increase in relation to inflation. All the interested parties — employers, unions and the Government — are brought before the Commission and then a judge delivers his verdict. This is the bedrock on which the Accord survives.

### Professional workers

Unions still have a great deal of influence — some people would say that they have too much. Workers who do not want to join a union can sign up with a professional association. These are related to professions such as doctors and lawyers and while they are not as powerful as the unions they can have an effective voice.

## SICK LEAVE

Australian employees are entitled to one or two weeks' fully paid sick leave a year, depending again on the award in their profession. Most people take full advantage of this allowance and hence the national habit of the 'sickie' — people taking time off even if they are not sick — has developed. This has become such a problem that the Government has recently commissioned a study into the problem. Recent research has shown that 16 per cent of workplaces with five or more employees have between 10 and 25 per cent of their workers away each day. The sickie is less prevalent in industries which have high levels of dismissals and it is most common among public servants.

## SUPERANNUATION

This is another scheme which was introduced as a bargaining tool to persuade trade unions to accept moderate wage increases. Under current legislation employers have to contribute at least three per cent of an employee's salary into an **approved superannuation fund**. This is a legal requirement for employers and they are liable to fines if the correct payments are not made.

All superannuation schemes are controlled closely and are included in different award arrangements. All employees are entitled to this form of award-based superannuation. These are some of the conditions:

- It must be three per cent of your average monthly wage, paid into a special fund by your employer.

- Failure to pay it by your employer is equivalent to failing to pay the correct wages.
- Award-based superannuation is paid to you from the time you begin

work. If your employer is not meeting his/her superannuation obligations you are entitled to a back-payment.

- Superannuation schemes are portable and you do not lose your payments if you change jobs or professions.

- You receive a payout from your superannuation fund when you reach 55 years of age.

- You can choose the type of scheme into which your superannuation is paid.

- If you are self-employed, or you are not part of a recognised superannuation scheme, you can contribute to more than one scheme if you wish.

- In certain cases, tax relief can be claimed against superannuation payments. For specific details contact a tax agent or an accountant.

In the past few years the Australian Government has promoted superannuation because it fears that, due to the aging population, future governments will not be able to afford to pay suitable pensions to retirees. A Government spokesman outlined the importance of superannuation, 'Superannuation is not the exclusive option it used to be. It is taking its place in broad incomes policy.

'It is no longer just a tax-advantaged privilege for a minority. It is part of the social wage, which means it is part of social policy. Workers have paid for their superannuation entitlements by accepting lower wages. Superannuation is deferred income held in trust until it matures.'

## FRINGE BENEFITS

The existence of fringe benefits in the Australian economy has declined steeply in recent years, due largely to the introduction of a **Fringe Benefits Tax** (FBT). This is levied on employers at the rate of 47 per cent of the taxable value of fringe benefits offered to employees. These benefits include such things as company cars which are also used for private purposes, expense accounts and private health plans. Because of this high level of taxation the most likely form of 'benefits' that employees can expect are subsidised canteens, living away from home allowances and superannuation deals. Since these are all covered by union awards they are not liable to FBT.

## WORKERS' COMPENSATION

Known universally as **compo** this is another prominent feature of the Australian employment landscape. Every accident in the workplace is taken very seriously and workers are invariably paid compensation to cover their medical expenses and their loss of earnings. The system is designed to protect the well-being of employees and because of this the worker is usually deemed to be in the right. He does not necessarily need to prove that his employer was negligent and it does not even matter if he was partly negligent himself.

Each state has its own legislation to cover compensation but they do not vary greatly. If a claim for compensation is rejected then the worker can take his case to a relevant union and the case will be heard before a workers' compensation commission or board.

## CONTRACTS OF EMPLOYMENT

Contracts of employment in Australia can be anything from a rough handshake from a fruit farmer, to a lengthy document from a multinational firm, to a simple public service contract. In some types of work you may not even be offered a formal contract but if you are there are some areas which you should check:

- rate of pay;
- hours of employment;
- holiday entitlement;
- whether you will be working flexi-time or not;
- overtime and penalty rates of pay;
- meal breaks;
- compensation provisions;
- provision of uniform/protective clothing;
- period of notice required from either party;
- rates of severance pay;
- superannuation contributions;
- specific rules and regulations;
- sick leave;
- sick pay;
- trade union membership;

- provision of private medical insurance;
- provision of a company car;
- pension contributions.;

In most jobs, even if part-time (or casual as it is frequently called), you should be offered some sort of contract. If nothing else this will guarantee you some form of payment in the event of employment being terminated abruptly. If you are not offered a written contract then ask for one. It may only be a simple sheet of paper but make sure that you and your employer sign something. Of course there are some areas where you will not be offered a contract. The most obvious is fruit-picking, a job notorious for its lack of control over working conditions. The chances are that you will be at the mercy of your employer but due to the nature of the work and conditions this will probably not be of prime importance.

If you are unhappy with any part of your contract then you should take it to a legal representative or trade union body.

# 4

## Problems in the Workplace

### SICKNESS

Australian workers are well provided for in the event of illness and there are two main areas they can guard against financial losses as a result of illness:

1.  Medicare.

2.  Private health plans.

### Medicare

Medicare is a form of national health insurance available to every resident of Australia, including temporary residents. You should apply to join Medicare as soon as you arrive in the country. You will need to fill in an application form for a Medicare card and these forms are available at all Medicare offices.

Medicare is partially financed by a tax on all taxable income, which is deducted at source. At present this stands at 1.5 per cent. Once you have joined Medicare it does not mean that you will be entitled to limitless, free medical treatment. It covers basic health needs such as visits to general practitioners, specialists and anaesthetists. However, Medicare only covers 85 per cent of these costs and the remaining 15 per cent usually has to be met by the patient. In most cases the full charge will be levied on the patient and then they will have to claim back the 85 per cent from Medicare.

Medicare also entitles patients to a general ward in a public hospital. However, for operations of a non life-threatening nature, such as hip replacements, there are long waiting-lists and it could be several months until there is a vacancy. Any treatment at a public hospital as a Medicare patient will be free but you will have to show your Medicare card.

## Private health insurance

Whether or not to take out private health insurance is very much up to the individual. Medicare is more than adequate for general health needs, but if you think you may need a lot of non-urgent medical attention then private health insurance may be a good idea. But before you commit yourself to the expense of a private plan look around at the various schemes on offer and see which one would suit you the best. Several companies, including **Medibank, ANA** and **HBA**, offer a variety of health plans and they should be consulted before any final decision is made. It is worth remembering that any illness has to be weighed against not only the medical costs but also the loss of earning from being off work for perhaps an extended period of time. The average weekly costs, per family, for private health insurance is in the region of $20-30.

In recent years there has been a big push to persuade people to take out private health insurance in Australia and there have even been some financial inventives to do this. Increasingly, companies are offering their employees membership to private health insurance plans.

## SEXUAL HARASSMENT

Although Australia has gone some way to shed its image of a beer-swilling, macho society, sexual harassment can nevertheless be a problem in the workplace. It is classed as:

● Any unwelcome sexual advance or request for sexual favours, or unwelcome conduct of a sexual nature.

It may include some of the following:

● An unwelcome comments or questions about a person's sex life;
● suggestive behaviour;
● over-familiarity such as deliberately brushing against someone;
● sexual jokes, offensive telephone calls, photographs, reading matter or objects;
● sexual propositions or continual requests for dates;
● physical contact such as touching, fondling, or unwanted sexual advances.

Although both men and women can be victims of sexual harassment it is usually the latter who are subjected to this type of discrimination. Since the Australian **Sex Discrimination Act 1984** much of this type of behaviour is now illegal and action can be taken against offenders. At its most extreme sexual harassment can take the form of rape or indecent assault. Since these are criminal offences they should be reported to the police.

Sexual harassment in the workplace is unlawful if:

1.  You have reasonable grounds for believing that your rejection of it will effect your application for a position, your current job or your future at work.

2.  You object to sexual harassment and are then unfairly treated by denial of a job or promotion, sacked, demoted or subjected to further harassment.

Under the Sex Discrimination Act management is obliged to prevent sexual harassment. The employer may be responsible if reasonable steps are not taken to prevent sexual harassment in the workplace.

## What can be done?

There are a number of steps that can be followed if you are subjected to sexual harassment at work:

● Make your objections to your supervisor and the person who is harassing you. If this proves to be the same person then take your complaint to a higher authority.

● Check to see if your company and its management has a policy to combat harassment. If not, then lobby to have one created.

● Complain to higher management.

● Seek help from your union.

● Look outside your place of employment for help. Seek a trustworthy counsellor for support and advice about solving the situation.

● Contact the Human Rights and Equal Opportunities Commission or a co-operating agency, where your problem will be dealt with in strictest confidence.

● Keep a record of when and where harassment takes place and do not be dissuaded from tackling the problem.

## The Sex Discrimination Commissioner

The **Human Rights and Equal Opportunity Commission** is responsible for administering the Sex Discrimination Act. The Sex Discrimination Commissioner exercises certain statutory powers of inquiry, conciliation and settlement of sex discrimination complaints on behalf of the Commission. Conciliation is the avenue used in most cases and this is the favoured approach of the Commission.

If you feel you are being sexually harassed you should contact your nearest Commission office or agency and explain the problem to them. They will be able to advise you as to whether you have lawful grounds for making a complaint. You will then be required to submit your complaint in writing before further action can be taken.

### Commission Offices

The national office is in Sydney and there are also regional offices in Brisbane, Hobart and Darwin. Complaints under Federal law in New South Wales, Victoria, South Australia and Western Australia are handled on behalf of the commission by the NSW Anti-Discrimination Board and the Equal Opportunity Commissioners in individual states. For the Australian Capital Territory complaints should be made in writing to the Commission's Sydney office:

Commission National Office: Level 24, American Express Building, 388 George Street, Sydney, NSW 2000. Postal address: GPO Box 5218, Sydney, NSW 2000. Tel: (02) 229 7600.

## RACIAL DISCRIMINATION

In 1975 the **Racial Discrimination Act** was passed. This prohibits discrimination in employment on the grounds of race, colour, descent or national or ethnic origin.

## REDUNDANCY

The thought of redundancy is never a pleasant one but in recent years it has become a more common problem. As firms seek to cut costs they 'rationalise' their operation, which invariably means shedding staff.

The good news is that the Australian Government has laid down guidelines covering payment and conditions covering redundancy. If the worst comes to the worst then people with a period of service with their company will be eligible for severance payments. These rules were set out in 1984 following the Termination Change and Redundancy (TCR) test case and they have recently been confirmed by the Confederation of Australian Industry (CAI). They define redundancy as, 'where an employer has made a definite decision that the employer no longer wishes the job the employee has been doing done by anyone, and this is not due to the ordinary and customary turnover of labour.'

The conditions governing severance pay and periods of notice are both laid down in relation to the length of service by the employee. However, the level of severance pay is not to exceed the amount the employee would have earned if they remained in employment until their normal retirement date.

The TCR ruling also states that after redundancies have been announced employers must allow their employees one day off a week in order to seek alternative employment. Employers must also notify the Centrelink, telling them the number of proposed redundancies, the categories of employees likely to be affected, the period over which the redundancies will occur and also provide employees with a 'statement of employment'.

If an employee receives a superannuation payment when he or she is made redundant then this will be counted against the amount of severance pay; they will receive the full sum less the amount received in superannuation.

The CAI concluded that the TCR test case should be used as a maximum and minimum standard and they stated that it is highly unlikely that any employer would be required to pay more than the levels of severance pay laid down in the test case.

## Period of notice

| *Period of continuous service* | *Notice in weeks* |
|---|---|
| One year or less | one |
| One year to three years | two |
| Three years to five years | three |
| Five years and over | four |

## Severance pay

| *Period of continuous service* | *Severance pay in weeks* |
|---|---|
| One year or less | nil |
| One year to two years | four |
| Two years to three years | six |
| Three years to four years | seven |
| Four years and over | eight |

● Employees over forty-five years of age and with more than two years service are entitled to an extra week's notice or pay in lieu of notice. All severance pay is at ordinary-time rates.

## STRIKES AND INDUSTRIAL DISPUTES

If you are involved in an industrial dispute and you are unable to work then you may be eligible to get help from the Department of Social Security. If you are a member of a trade union then you will probably not receive any state benefits — you will have to see your union to see what provisions they make for workers on strike. However, you will receive unemployment benefit if:

● you have been sacked as a result of an industrial dispute which is now over;
● you have been sacked or stood down in an industrial dispute that your union is not part of.

If your spouse is a member of a union involved in an industrial dispute, you can get paid unemployment benefit for yourself and your dependent children. However, you will not be paid for your spouse.

## WORKING ILLEGALLY

There are currently approximately 80,000 illegal immigrants in Australia and it is thought that 60 per cent of them are working illegally. Of this total it is estimated that 8.3 per cent are British. Obviously, people who have migrated to Australia will not make up any of this number but it is thought that people overstaying their holiday working visas account for a large number of the British illegal immigrants. The rest are those who have travelled on tourist visas and decided to stay.

Understandably, the Australian Government is becoming increasingly frustrated by the number of illegal immigrants, and particularly those who are taking jobs away from legitimate workers.

A new policy was introduced in 2000 designed to discourage employers taking on illegal workers. The penalties for this include fines of up to $A66,000 and up to two years imprisonment. Philip Ruddock, the then Minister for Immigration, said the Government would make it easier to clamp down on people who were working illegally, 'We propose to make the system easier for employers to check whether someone is working illegally, through the use of information and support services.

We will also undertake a revised employer awareness campaign to ensure employers are aware of their obligations.' The Minister went on to say, 'Responsible Australian businesses should not be disadvantaged when competitors recruit illegal workers to undercut the labour market and bypass proper immigration processes. The new sanctions will mean greater employment opportunities for Australians and those who have a right to work, while making Australia a less attractive target for illegal workers.'

The message to people who are thinking of overstaying their visas and working illegally in Australia is *don't*. It is increasingly likely that you will be caught, in which case you will probably be unceremoniously deported and not made welcome if you ever try and return.

# 5

## Finance

### TAX

Even in the 'Lucky Country' this three letter word is inescapable. The tax year runs from 1st July to 30th June and it pays (sometimes literally) to have a good understanding of the tax system.

For people whose income comes from a salary or a wage, tax is levied through a **Pay As You Go** (PAYG) system which is known as **standard rate taxation**. However, the story does not end there because the tax payer has to step daintily through a minefield of Tax File Numbers, Tax Forms, Tax Packs, deductions and refunds.

#### Your Tax File Number (TFN)
The most important thing for migrants to consider is that it is *vital* to obtain a Tax File Number as soon as possible upon entering Australia. This is a number which needs to be quoted whenever you apply for a job or fill in the dreaded income tax return. If you do not have one then you will be taxed at the top rate of 47 per cent. You will be able to claim some of this back but you will have to wait until the end of the tax year to do so.

Tax File Numbers can be obtained by filling in an application form available from the Post Office or the local tax office. To do this you will have to have proof of your identity — birth certificate, passport (including residency visa) and driving licence.

#### Tax Reform
On 1 July 2000 a new Tax System came into effect. This includes a new goods and services tax (GST), a $12 billion cut in personal income tax, increases in government benefits (such as the age pension and family assistance), a one-off bonus for seniors, the abolition of wholesale sales tax, and the abolition of provisional tax.

#### GST
The GST is a broad-based tax of 10 per cent on most goods and services.

GST is included in the price of goods and services. For each product or service, GST will effectively only be paid once – in the final price. The slight increase in some prices due to the inclusion of GST is generally offset by the new tax rates and the abolition of various hidden taxes.

## Rates of tax (from 1 July 2000)

| Taxable income | Tax |
| --- | --- |
| $A0–6000 | Nil |
| $A6,001–20,000 | 17% |
| $A20,001–50,000 | 30% |
| $A50,001–60,000 | 42% |
| $A60,001+ | 47% |

For information about the new tax system and the overall tax system, take a look at the following Web sites:
www.ato.gov.au/

These rates do not include the Medicare levy of 1.5 per cent, and apply to people who have been resident in Australia for the full financial year.

### Tax forms and tax pack

All taxpayers in Australia, even if you are a PAYG employee, are required to fill in a tax form at the end of the financial year. In simple terms (nothing about tax forms is ever simple of course) this involves declaring all of your taxable income and also noting any expenses you can claim against your tax. The form for this is something akin to a small encyclopedia — but help is at hand. The Tax Office issues a 116 page booklet entitled *Tax Pack*; this not only includes four copies of tax return forms but also offers invaluable information about filling in your tax form. The scale of the task can be seen from the fact that the front of the Tax Pack declares merrily, 'You don't have to read all of Tax Pack'. In fairness it does take you through the whole operation step by step.

● Tax forms must be completed and returned by **31st October** for the previous tax year. Failure to do so could result in financial penalties.

### Tax agents

When it comes to the time of year for filling in the tax form you can tell who has chosen to fill them in themselves and who has entrusted them

**1999 TAX RETURN FOR INDIVIDUALS**

Australian Taxation Office

Use *TaxPack 99* to fill in this tax return. Do not use correction fluid or tape.
Please print neatly in BLOCK LETTERS with a black or blue ballpoint pen only.
Print one letter or number in each box. Print ⊠ in appropriate boxes.

▶ **Your tax file number (TFN)**

See the **Privacy** note in the *Taxpayer's declaration* on page 6 of this tax return.

▶ **Are you an Australian resident?**
See page 8 of *TaxPack 99*.   YES ☐   NO ☐

▶ **Your sex**   Male ☐   Female ☐

▶ **Your name**   Title—for example, Mr, Mrs, Ms, Miss
Print your full name.

▶ **Has any part of your name changed since completing your last tax return?**   Surname or family name

Given names

NO ☐   YES ☐ ──▶ Previous surname

▶ **Your postal address**
Print the address where you want your mail sent.

▶ **Has this address changed since completing your last tax return?**
Fill in the appropriate box then go to the next question.   Suburb or town

State ☐ Postcode ☐ Country *if not Australia*

NO ☐   YES ☐

▶ **Is your home address different from your postal address?**

NO ☐ *Go to the next question.*
YES ☐ *Print your home address.*   Suburb or town

State ☐ Postcode ☐ Country *if not Australia*

▶ **Your date of birth**
If you were under 18 years of age on 30 June 1999 you must complete item A1 on this tax return. Read page 100 of *TaxPack 99* for more information.   Day Month Year

Please provide your date of birth to avoid delays in the processing of your tax return.

▶ **Your daytime telephone number**—please write your telephone number if it is convenient.
If we need to ask you about your tax return, it is quicker by telephone.
Area code ☐ Telephone number ☐

▶ **Your spouse's name**
If you had more than one spouse during 1998–99 print the name of your latest spouse.   Surname or family name

Given names

▶ **Will you need to lodge an Australian tax return in the future?**   YES ☐   DON'T KNOW ☐   NO ☐ FINAL

| ATO use only | |
|---|---|
| ETP 5% | B |
| ETP1—Code | C |
| ETP1—Lrt | D |
| ETP1—Hrt | E |
| ETP2—Code | I |
| ETP2—Lrt | Q |
| ETP2—Hrt | R |
| Average code | H |
| Indicators | X |
| LLP-Start | S |
| LLP-End | T |
| M/I indicators | P |

▶ **Do you want to use electronic funds transfer (EFT) for your refund this year?**
Read page 10 of *TaxPack 99* for more information.

NO ☐ *Go to page 2.*
YES ☐ If you used EFT last year and the account details you provided are correct, do not write them again.

BSB number ☐   Account number ☐

Account name—for example, JQ Citizen. Do not show the account type, such as cheque, savings, mortgage offset.

IN-CONFIDENCE—when completed   PAGE 1 ▶

Fig. 2. Sample Tax Forms.

## Income
*TaxPack 99 pages 13–32 will help you to correctly fill in the following items.*

**1  Salary or wages**

Your main salary and wage occupation

Description

| Name of employer | Tax instalments deducted—show cents | | Income—do not show cents |
|---|---|---|---|
| | | **C** | ·00 |
| | | **D** | ·00 |
| | | **E** | ·00 |
| | | **F** | ·00 |
| | | **G** | ·00 |

**2  Allowances, earnings, tips, director's fees, etc.** — **K** ·00

**3  Lump sum payments**
Amount A in lump sum payments box — **R** ·00
5% of amount B in lump sum payments box — **H** ·00

**4  Eligible termination payments**
Taxable amount other than excessive component — **I** ·00
Attach the originals of your statements of termination payment, any roll-over payment notifications and your copy of any group certificates or letters to page 3 of your tax return.
Excessive component — **N** ·00

**5  Commonwealth of Australia government allowances and payments like Newstart, youth allowance and austudy payment** — **A** ·00

**6  Commonwealth of Australia government pensions and allowances** — **B** ·00  REBATE □ CODE

If you had a spouse during 1998–99 and you have written either code letter **A** or **M** in the REBATE CODE box, complete Spouse details—married or de facto on page 6.

**7  Other Australian pensions or annuities—including superannuation pensions**

Type — **J** ·00

**TOTAL TAX INSTALMENTS DEDUCTED** **S** ·00 ◄ For items 1 to 7 add up all the amounts in the tax instalments deducted column.

**8  Gross interest** *If you are a non-resident make sure you have printed your country of residence on page 1.* Gross interest **L** ·00
TFN amounts deducted from gross interest **M** ·

**9  Dividends** Unfranked amount **S** ·00
*If you are a non-resident make sure you have printed your country of residence on page 1.* Franked amount **T** ·00
Imputation credit **U** ·00
TFN amounts deducted from dividends **V** ·

**I** Only used by taxpayers completing the *1999 tax return for individuals* (supplementary section)
Transfer the amount from TOTAL SUPPLEMENT INCOME OR LOSS on page 9 and write it here. ·00

**TOTAL INCOME OR LOSS** Add up all the income amounts and deduct any loss amount in the right-hand column. **S** ·00

Make sure that you complete item M2. See pages 94–8 in *TaxPack 99*.

Fig. 2. (continued).

Attach your employee's tax return copy of group certificates, any income tax credit vouchers and other requested attachments here. Place your group certificates on top, followed by any other attachments.

Do not send in this tax return until you have attached all your group certificates and any other requested attachments.

**1999 Group Certificate** — Australian Taxation Office, Income Year 1 July 1998 to 30 June 1999

| Item 1 → Name of Employer | Tax File Number → Page 1 |

Item 1, 2 or 7
Item 2
Item 3
Item 4
Items 1 to 7

Item D5 — Union Fees, etc.

---

## Deductions
*TaxPack 99 pages 33–59 will help you to correctly claim all your deductions.*

You must read *TaxPack 99* pages 34–5 if you are claiming deductions for expenses that relate to your work as an employee at items D1, D2, D3, D4 or D5.

Deductions—do not show cents

| D1 | Work related car expenses | A | .00 | CLAIM TYPE |
| D2 | Work related travel expenses | B | .00 | |
| D3 | Work related uniform, occupation specific or protective clothing, laundry and dry cleaning expenses | C | .00 | CLAIM TYPE |
| D4 | Work related self-education expenses | D | .00 | CLAIM TYPE |
| D5 | Other work related expenses | E | .00 | |
| D6 | Interest and dividend deductions | I | .00 | |
| D7 | Gifts or donations | J | .00 | CLAIM TYPE |
| D8 | Deductible amount of undeducted purchase price (UPP) of *Australian* pension or annuity. Deductible amount of UPP of foreign pensions or annuities must be claimed at item D12 on page 10 of the tax return (supplementary section). | L | .00 | |
| D9 | Cost of managing tax affairs | M | .00 | |
| D | Only used by taxpayers completing the *1999 tax return for individuals* (supplementary section) — Transfer the amount from **TOTAL SUPPLEMENT DEDUCTIONS** on page 10 and write it here. | | .00 | |

**TOTAL DEDUCTIONS** — Add up all the deduction amounts. .00

**TAXABLE INCOME OR LOSS** — Subtract TOTAL DEDUCTIONS from TOTAL INCOME OR LOSS. **S** .00

Don't forget to sign the *Taxpayer's declaration* on page 6. PAGE 3 ►

Fig. 2. (continued).

## Rebates
*TaxPack 99 pages 61–86 will help you to correctly claim your rebates.*

**R1** **Spouse—married or de facto—child-housekeeper or housekeeper**
To claim the spouse rebate you must also complete **Spouse details—married or de facto** on page 6. Separate net income of your spouse must be shown at page 6, not here.

Rebates—do not show cents

Child-housekeeper's separate net income **V** ⬚,⬚⬚⬚.00    Basic parenting payment (partnered) **W** ⬚,⬚⬚⬚.00    **P** ⬚,⬚⬚⬚.00 CLAIM TYPE

**R2** **Sole parent**    **Q** ⬚,⬚⬚⬚.00 CLAIM TYPE

**R3** **Low income aged person**
If you had a spouse during 1998–99 you must also complete **Spouse details—married or de facto** on page 6.
**N** ⬚ The ATO will work out this rebate. Print your code letter here. Read pages 71–2 in *TaxPack 99*.

**R4** **Superannuation contributions, annuity and pension**
Personal undeducted superannuation contributions **T** ⬚⬚⬚,⬚⬚⬚.00    Superannuation contributions, annuity and pension rebates **S** ⬚,⬚⬚⬚.00 CLAIM TYPE
The ATO will use the amount you show at **T** to calculate your **savings rebate**.
See page 73 in *TaxPack 99* for more information.

*TaxPack 99 pages 76–85 will help you to correctly fill in items R5 and R6.*

**R5** **Private health insurance incentive—from 1 July to 31 December 1998**
Number of dependent children covered by the policy **R** ⬚⬚    Amount of rebate—not contributions **F** ⬚⬚⬚.00
You **must** complete **Private health insurance policy details** below.
If you had a spouse during 1998–99 you must also complete **Spouse details—married or de facto** on page 6.

**R6** **30% private health insurance rebate—from 1 January 1999**
Amount of refundable rebate—not contributions **G** ⬚,⬚⬚⬚.00
You **must** complete **Private health insurance policy details** below.

**R** Only used by taxpayers completing the *1999 tax return for individuals* (supplementary section)
Transfer the amount from **TOTAL SUPPLEMENT REBATES** on page 10 and write it here. ⬚⬚,⬚⬚⬚.00

**TOTAL REBATES**    Add up the rebate amounts in the right-hand column. **U** $ ⬚⬚,⬚⬚⬚.00

The ATO will work out any rebate for low income. Read page 86 of *TaxPack 99* for more information.

## Private health insurance policy details
*TaxPack 99 pages 87–8 will help you to correctly fill in your details.*

If items R5, R6 or M2 asked you to complete this section, or you made premium payments towards private health insurance, you must provide the details for each policy.

| Health fund ID | Membership number | Type of cover |
|---|---|---|
| **B** ⬚⬚⬚ | **C** ⬚⬚⬚⬚⬚⬚⬚⬚⬚⬚⬚⬚⬚⬚⬚ | ⬚ |
| **B** ⬚⬚⬚ | **C** ⬚⬚⬚⬚⬚⬚⬚⬚⬚⬚⬚⬚⬚⬚⬚ | ⬚ |
| **B** ⬚⬚⬚ | **C** ⬚⬚⬚⬚⬚⬚⬚⬚⬚⬚⬚⬚⬚⬚⬚ | ⬚ |

## Medicare levy related items
*TaxPack 99 pages 89–98 will help you to correctly fill in these items.*

**M1** **Medicare levy reduction or exemption**
If you had a spouse during 1998–99 you must also complete **Spouse details—married or de facto** on page 6.
Only certain taxpayers are entitled to a Medicare levy reduction or exemption. Read pages 90–3 of *TaxPack 99* to work out if you are eligible to claim.

*Reduction based on family income*
Number of dependent children and students **Y** ⬚⬚

*Exemption categories*
Full 1.5% levy exemption—number of days **V** ⬚⬚⬚ CLAIM TYPE
Half 1.5% levy exemption—number of days **W** ⬚⬚⬚

Fig. 2. (continued).

## Medicare levy related items—*continued*

**M2** Medicare levy surcharge [STOP] **THIS ITEM IS COMPULSORY FOR ALL TAXPAYERS.** If you do not complete this item you may be charged the full Medicare levy surcharge.

To help you determine if you have to pay the surcharge read pages 94–8 of *TaxPack 99*.
Were **you** and all of your dependants—including your spouse—covered by private patient HOSPITAL cover for the **whole** period 1 July 1998 to 30 June 1999?

**E** **NO** ☐ Read below.  **YES** ☐ You **must** complete **Private health insurance policy details** on page 4. You have now finished this item.

Were you:
- **single** for the WHOLE of 1998–99—without dependent children—and your taxable income for MLS purposes was $50 000 or less **OR**
- a **family** for the WHOLE of 1998–99—including a sole parent—and the combined taxable income for MLS purposes of you and your spouse was $100 000 (plus $1500 for each dependent child after the first) or less?

**NO** ☐ You may have to pay the surcharge— read pages 94–6 of *TaxPack 99*.  **YES** ☐ You do not have to pay the surcharge— you **must** write '365' at **A**.

You must write the following at **A**:
- '0' when you have to pay the surcharge for the whole period 1 July 1998 to 30 June 1999
- '365' when you do NOT have to pay the surcharge for the whole period 1 July 1998 to 30 June 1999
- the **number of days** you do NOT have to pay the surcharge for part of the period 1 July 1998 to 30 June 1999

→ Number of days you do NOT have to pay the surcharge **A** ☐☐☐

Number of dependent children **D** ☐☐

If you had a spouse during 1998–99 complete **Spouse details—married or de facto** on page 6.
If you were covered by private patient hospital cover during 1998–99 you **must** complete **Private health insurance policy details** on page 4.

## Adjustments  *TaxPack 99* pages 99–109 will help you to correctly fill in these items.

**A1** Under 18 excepted net income  **J** ☐☐☐,☐☐☐ ·00 ☐ TYPE

**A2** Part-year tax-free threshold
Date ☐☐ ☐☐ ☐☐☐☐
Day  Month  Year
Months eligible for threshold **N** ☐☐
Income while a full-time student **O** ☐☐,☐☐☐ ·00

**A3** Amount on which family trust distribution tax has been paid
If a trust, partnership or company made a distribution to you on which family trust distribution tax has been paid, you **must** read page 103 in *TaxPack 99*.
**X** ☐☐☐,☐☐☐ ·00

**A4** Family tax assistance
[CAUTION] Only complete this item if you are eligible for family tax assistance (FTA).
Read pages 104–9 of *TaxPack 99* for more information.
If you had a spouse during 1998–99 you must also complete **Spouse details—married or de facto** on page 6.

**Details of dependants for FTA purposes**
For FTA purposes, each dependent child must:
- be under 18 during 1998–99 AND
- meet the income test explained on pages 104–6 of *TaxPack 99*.

| Given names of FTA dependants | | Date of birth | | | FULL care Number of nights | | SHARED care single period Number of nights you provided care | | SHARED care single period Number of nights others provided care | | SHARED care multiple periods Number of nights you provided care | |
|---|---|---|---|---|---|---|---|---|---|---|---|---|
| | | Day | Month | Year | | | | | | | | |
| 1 | **A** | ☐☐ | ☐☐ | ☐☐☐☐ | **B** | ☐☐☐ | **C** | ☐☐☐ | **D** | ☐☐☐ | **E** | ☐☐☐ |
| 2 | **A** | ☐☐ | ☐☐ | ☐☐☐☐ | **B** | ☐☐☐ | **C** | ☐☐☐ | **D** | ☐☐☐ | **E** | ☐☐☐ |
| 3 | **A** | ☐☐ | ☐☐ | ☐☐☐☐ | **B** | ☐☐☐ | **C** | ☐☐☐ | **D** | ☐☐☐ | **E** | ☐☐☐ |
| 4 | **A** | ☐☐ | ☐☐ | ☐☐☐☐ | **B** | ☐☐☐ | **C** | ☐☐☐ | **D** | ☐☐☐ | **E** | ☐☐☐ |
| 5 | **A** | ☐☐ | ☐☐ | ☐☐☐☐ | **B** | ☐☐☐ | **C** | ☐☐☐ | **D** | ☐☐☐ | **E** | ☐☐☐ |

Maximum number of FTA dependent children cared for at any one time from 1 July 1998 to 30 June 1999 inclusive **F** ☐

Number of nights you provided care for one or more dependent children under 5 years of age from 1 July 1998 to 30 June 1999 inclusive—a maximum of 365 nights. If more than one child under 5 do not count the same night more than once. **G** ☐☐☐

**Family tax payment details**
Amount of family tax payment received from Centrelink for the dependent children for whom you are claiming FTA. The family tax payment may have been received by you, your spouse, or another person living with you.
Part A **H** ☐☐,☐☐☐ ·00
Part B **I** ☐☐☐ ·00

PAGE 5 ▶

Fig. 2. (continued).

If you are completing the supplementary section (pages 7–10) of your tax return — attach it here. ⟶ ●

## Spouse details — married or de facto

Only provide these details if you had a spouse — married or de facto — during 1998–99 and you completed any of the following items:

| | |
|---|---|
| 6 | Commonwealth of Australia government pensions and allowances |
| R1 | spouse rebate |
| R3 | low income aged person rebate |
| R5 | private health insurance incentive — from 1 July to 31 December 1998 |

| | |
|---|---|
| M1 | Medicare levy reduction or exemption |
| M2 | Medicare levy surcharge — and you printed X in the NO box at label E |
| A4 | family tax assistance |
| R7 | superannuation contributions on behalf of your spouse rebate |

**Privacy** — It is not an offence not to quote your spouse's tax file number (TFN). However, the TFN will help us to process your claim. The TFN may be used to confirm your spouse's income. If you cannot provide the TFN, please provide your spouse's date of birth.

Spouse's tax file number — only complete if you are claiming family tax assistance  **J**

Spouse's date of birth  **K**
Day  Month  Year

Did you have a spouse for the full year — 1 July 1998 to 30 June 1999?  **L**  YES ☐  NO ☐

If you did not have a spouse for the full year, write the dates you had a spouse between 1 July 1998 and 30 June 1999.  **M**  From
Day  Month  Year

**N**  To
Day  Month  Year

You only need to complete spouse's taxable income if:
– you had a spouse on 30 June 1999 AND you completed one or more of items R5, M1 (label V only) and A4
– you had a spouse for all of 1998–99 AND you printed X in the NO box at label E item M2
– you had a spouse for any part of the year AND you completed one or more of items 6, R3, R7 and M1 (label V or W).

Spouse's 1998–99 taxable income. You must provide your spouse's taxable income. Otherwise we cannot determine your rebate entitlement. If your spouse's income is zero, write '0'.  **O** .00

If you completed item A4 show the amount of any Commonwealth of Australia government payments — listed at questions 5 or 6 in TaxPack 99 — included in your spouse's taxable income. Do not include family tax payment.  **P** .00

If you completed item 6 show the amount of any exempt pension income — see page 12 of TaxPack 99 — received by your spouse in 1998–99.  **Q** .00

If you completed item R1 show your spouse's 1998–99 separate net income — see page 63 of TaxPack 99.  **R** .00

## Taxpayer's declaration

Read and answer the questions below before you sign the Taxpayer's declaration.

**1. Are you required to complete any of the items in the 1999 tax return for individuals (supplementary section) — pages 7 to 10? Read page 5 in TaxPack 99 to find out.**

NO ☐ Go to question 2.    YES ☐ Attach pages 7–10 (including any attachments) to this page.

**2. Has TaxPack asked you to attach the following?**

a. any attachments relating to specific questions — either to page 3 or page 9    NO ☐  YES ☐

b. 1999 business and professional items schedule — to page 9    NO ☐  YES ☐

These attachments are in addition to your group certificates and other income statements which you must attach to your tax return.

**Privacy**

It is not an offence not to quote your tax file number (TFN). However, your TFN helps the Australian Taxation Office (ATO) to correctly identify your tax records.

The ATO is authorised by the Income Tax Assessment Act 1936 and the Income Tax Assessment Act 1997 to ask for information in this tax return. We need this information to help us to administer the tax laws.

We may give some of this information to other government agencies authorised by law to receive it, including Centrelink and the departments of Family and Community Services; Veterans' Affairs; and Education, Training and Youth Affairs.

**I declare that:**
- all the information I have given in this tax return, including any attachments, is true and correct
- I have shown all my income — including net capital gains — for tax purposes from sources in and out of Australia for 1998–99
- I have completed and attached the supplementary section, schedules and other attachments — as appropriate — that TaxPack told me to provide
- I have completed item M2 — Medicare levy surcharge
- I have the necessary receipts and/or other records — or expect to obtain the necessary written evidence within a reasonable time of lodging this tax return — to support my claims for deductions, rebates and family tax assistance AND
- I have obtained the consent of my spouse to quote their tax file number.

**Important**

If you are not an Australian resident, you may delete the words and out of from the declaration.

**The tax law imposes heavy penalties for giving false or misleading information.**

SIGNATURE

Date ☐☐ ☐☐ ☐☐☐☐
Day  Month  Year

NAT 2541 – 6.1999

**Where to lodge? Read page 136 in TaxPack 99.**

Fig. 2. (continued).

to a **tax agent**. The freelancers wander around with worried expressions and furled brows, muttering about petrol allowances and taxable income. Those who have left it in the hands of an agent are usually to be found on the beach or on the golf course, looking forward to a possible refund. The truth of the matter is that you can fill in your own tax form but it is a lot easier, and more often than not a lot more profitable, to let the professionals do it.

Of course, tax agents charge a fee but for the average PAYG taxpayer this will be between $100-$150. Additional fees are charged for additional services but it is worth remembering that fees for tax agents can be claimed as tax deductible.

Apart from saving you lots of grey hairs the main advantage of using a tax agent is that they will be in the best position to try and get you a refund on the tax you have paid, rather than having to pay more. Agents will make sure that you claim for all the deductions to which you are entitled — one of the most common oversights by the individual is not claiming all their deductions. Some of the deductions which can be claimed are:

*Deductible expenses*
- union dues;
- car expenses (but not to or from your place of work);
- travel expenses;
- tools and equipment;
- uniforms and protective clothing;
- home laundry of uniforms;
- sickness/accident insurance premiums;
- self-education.

*Expenses over $300*
If your claims for work-related expenses exceed $300 you must keep records to prove your claim. These should include receipts with:
- the date on which the expense was incurred;
- the name of the person or business who supplied the goods or service;
- the amount of the expense;
- details of the goods or services;
- the date the document was made out.

For possible auditing purposes these receipts have to be kept for three-and-a-half-years by salary and wage earners and seven years for the self-employed.

Unless you are a financial wizard, or you actually *enjoy* filling in tax forms, it would probably be better to employ the services of a tax agent. They are generally cheaper than accountants, who tend to charge by the hour.

## Paying tax

After lodging your tax form you will receive a **Notice of Assessment**. The amount of tax due, if any, will be shown on this assessment, as will the date by which it should be paid.

When you come to the dreaded moment of paying your tax you can do so by taking it in by person or by posting it to the tax office which issued your Notice of Assessment. Cheques and postal orders should be made payable to the 'Deputy Commissioner of Taxation' and crossed 'not negotiable'. The bottom section of your assessment should be sent with your payment. If you cannot find it then you should include your name and address and, of course, your Tax File Number. Further details are available on the back of the Notice of Assessment.

### Late payment of tax

If you feel you are unable to pay your tax by the due date you should write to your tax office immediately, explaining your circumstances. This should include:

- Your name and address.
- Your Tax File Number.
- Your work and telephone number.
- The reasons why you cannot pay your tax.
- How you plan to get the money to pay your tax.
- The amounts you can pay on a regular basis.
- Your first payment.
- The date by which you expect to have paid the full amount.

However, the tax office's charity does not extend to giving you an interest-free period in which to pay your tax: you will be charged an additional tax for late payment.

## Tax Offices

There are tax offices throughout Australia where you can get information about completing and returning your tax form. Use the one nearest to your area:

GPO Box 800, Adelaide, South Australia 5001 (also for Northern Territory).
PO Box 9990, Albury, NSW 2640.
GPO Box 9990, Brisbane, Queensland 4001.
GPO Box 9990, Canberra, ACT 2601.
PO Box 9990 Chatswood, NSW 2057.
PO Box 9990, Dandenong, Victoria 3175.
GPO Box 9990, Hobart, Tasmania 7001.
GPO Box 9990, Melbourne, Victoria 3001.
PO Box 9990, Moonee Ponds, Victoria 3039 (for Victoria North).
PO Box 9990, Newcastle, NSW 2300.
PO Box 9990, Parramatta, NSW 2123.
PO Box 9990, Penrith, NSW 2740.
GPO Box 9990, Sydney, NSW 2001.
GPO Box 9990, Perth, Western Australia 6001.
PO Box 9990, Townsville, Queensland 4810.

## Capital Gains Tax

This is a tax levied on any capital gain realised from the disposal of assets acquired after 19th September 1985. Gains made on the sale of the taxpayer's principal residence are usually exempt from Capital Gains Tax. Other items which are exempt are motor vehicles, superannuation and insurance, personal goods which have a disposable value of $A5,000 or less, and assets acquired before the 20th September 1985.

## SOCIAL SECURITY

Australia has one of the best social security systems in the world and in 1997 a new agency, Centrelink, was created to provide more services in the one place.

## CENTRELINK

Centrelink is a government agency that was launched in September 1997. Its aim is to streamline various aspects of Australia's public service so that more services are available in the one place, linking people to the services they need and for which they qualify.

Centrelink Customer Service Centres provide, under one roof, a range of customer services currently being delivered for:

- Department of Family and Community Services.
- Department of Education, Training and Youth Affairs.
- Department of Health and Aged Care.
- Department of Employment, Workplace Relations & Small Business.
- Department of Veterans' Affairs.
- Department of Agriculture, Fisheries & Forestry.
- Department of Transport and Regional Services.
- Department of Communication, Information Technology & the Arts.
- Tasmanian State Government.
- State & Territory Housing Authorities.

The services include:

- all services formerly provided by DSS offices, as well as childcare and student assistance payments and services;
- registration and acceptance of all new applicants for income support and employment assistance;
- self-help job search facilities, including computer access to a national job vacancies database;
- referrals for employment assistance;
- specialist labour market assistance services for disadvantaged groups, including Aboriginals and Torres Strait Islanders, sole parents, people with disabilities, migrants and young people.

## Programs and information services administered by Centrelink

For retired people or people planning retirement:

- Age Pension.
- Financial Information Service.
- Pensioner Concession Card.
- Commonwealth Seniors' Health Card.
- Pensioner Bonus Scheme.

For people in special circumstances:

- Disability Support Pension.
- Carer Payment.
- Sickness Allowance.
- Mobility Allowance.

- Carer Allowance.
- Postal Concessions for the Blind.
- Special Benefit.
- Bereavement Allowance.
- Bereavement Payments.
- Widow Allowance.
- Widow Pension Class B.
- Partner Allowance.
- Pensioner Concession Card.
- Farm Household Support.
- Drought Relief Payment.
- Disaster Relief Payment.
- Health Care Cards.
- Wife Pension.
- Remote Area Allowance.

For job seekers, students and young people:

- Youth Allowance.
- Austudy.
- ABSTUDY.
- Assistance for Isolated Children Scheme.
- Pensioner Education Supplement (PES).
- Loan Supplement (for the above payments).
- Newstart Allowance.
- Community Development Employment Projects (CDEP) Participants Supplement (CPS) and Supplementary Benefits (Add-Ons).
- Mature Age Allowance.
- Mature Age Partner Allowance.

For Families:

- Family Allowance.
- Family Tax Payment.
- Double Orphan Pension.
- Maternity Allowance.
- Parenting Payment.
- Jobs, Education and Training program.
- Maternity Immunisation Allowance.

Centrelink can be visited on the Web at: www.centrelink.gov.au/
The three main types of benefit that concern us here are:

- Age Pensions.
- Youth Training Allowance.
- Newstart.

## Age pensions

Age pensions are paid to men over 65 and women over 60. Under normal circumstances you must have been a resident of Australia for 10 years. However, special conditions apply and Australia has agreements with a number of countries where residence in one country can count towards residence in Australia. The United Kingdom is covered by this agreement.

Age pensions are assessed according to two criteria:

1. Income Test.
2. Assets Test.

*The Income Test*
Under the Income Test a full pension is paid to you if your gross income (not including maintenance) does not exceed $A120.00 a fortnight for a single pensioner and $A212.00 a fortnight (combined) for a pensioner couple. Income above these amounts reduces the pension payable by 50 cents for each dollar (single) and 25 cents in the dollar (each of a couple).

*The Assets Test*
Under the Assets Test you will receive a full pension if the current market value of your assessable assets totals less than the following:

| | |
|---|---|
| Single homeowner | $A149,500 |
| Single non-homeowner | $A257,500 |
| Married homeowner couple (combined) | $A212,500 |
| Married non-homeowner couple (combined) | $A320,500 |

If you receive any maintenance then this will affect your pension slightly differently than other income. You will get your full rate of payment if you receive less than $A936 per annum maintenance. This is increased by $A312 per annum for each child after your first. Maintenance above this allowable amount reduces your payment by 50 cents for each dollar.

*Pension rates and payment*

As of Sept 2003 the maximum fortnightly pension for a single person was $A450.80. For a married couple it was $A378.00 (each).

You can claim your pension shortly before you reach retirement age. You can get the relevant forms from any Social Security Regional Office and you will need proof of your identity — passport or driving licence is suitable for this. Your pension will be paid into your bank, building society or credit union account, every second Thursday.

## Youth Training Allowance

This is one payment made to unemployed people under the Newstart program.

Your payment will be assessed after an Income and an Assets test. The Assets test is the same as the one for age pensions. Under the Incomes test you will be paid the full rate if your gross income does not exceed $A62.00 a fortnight. For each dollar of income between $A62.00 and $A142.00 you will lose 50 cents from your rate. Income over $A142.00 reduces your rate by 50 cents per dollar.

When you apply for Youth Training Allowance you will need to take your Tax File Number and your **Employment Separation Certificate.** This comes from your last employer and relates why you left work and how much money you were paid.

You can receive your Youth Training Allowance every fortnight by taking a form to the CENTRELINK, detailing your efforts to find work. After this a payment is made into your bank, building society or credit union account. The rates vary according to age, marital status and number of children. The maximum rate for a single person over the age of 21, with no children, is currently $A376.00 a fortnight.

## Newstart Allowance

To be eligible for this you must be:

- unemployed;
- over 18 years of age;
- registered with the Centrelink;
- allowed to live in Australia permanently;
- actively searching for work.

Centrelink will apply an activity test to make sure that you are actively looking for work, or trying to improve your chances of getting some. These activities will be decided by the Centrelink. In addition you will have to report to the Centrelink every fortnight and update them about your job-hunting. Unless you have a good reason for not meeting the activity test your payment will be stopped.

In order to receive your allowance you will have to sign an **action plan** agreement with the Centrelink, which is aimed at improving your job prospects. The Newstart allowance is usually paid from the day after the Youth Training Allowance stops. The Income and Asset test are the same for both schemes, as are rates of payment.

## OTHER FINANCIAL MATTERS

Personal and business finances are one of the biggest worries when planning to work in another country. These worries have been addressed by the Commonwealth Bank of Australia. They not only offer various financial services before you arrive in Australia, such as opening overseas bank accounts and transferring money overseas, but they will also help you get settled when you step off the plane. This includes offering advice on general financial matters as they apply to Australia, such as buying a house, superannuation and investments. The Bank has Migrant Service Centres in each state capital and they also hold Migrant Information Days throughout major cities in Britain. For further information contact:

Financial and Migrant Information Service
3rd Floor, No. 1 Kingsway
London WC2B 6DU
Tel: (0207) 379 0955.

They will be able to provide you with an information pack and an invaluable book which covers a wide range of financial matters in Australia.

# 6

## The Official Recruitment Network

### CENTRELINK SERVICES

In addition to providing a variety of benefits payments, Centrelink also has offices around Australia that can provide information about local and national employment. These and the other services offered by Centrelink can be obtained by telephoning the following numbers: Appoints Tel: 13 1021.
To make an appointment to see someone in your local Centrelink office

Employment Services Tel: 13 2850.

Newstart allowance, Mature Age Allowance, Widow Allowance, Special Benefit, (Partner Allowance/Parenting Payment/Maintenance Enquiries: If your spouse receives one of these payments) Retirement Tel: 13 2300.

Age Pension, Pensioner Concession Cards, (Partner Allowance/Maintenance Enquiries: If your spouse receives one of these payments) Disability, Sickness and Carers Tel: 13 2717.

Disability Support Pension, Carer Payment, Mobility Sickness Allowance, Child Disability Allowance (Wife Pension Partner Allowance Parenting Payment of your spouse receives one of these payments) Families Tel: 13 1305.

Family Allowance, Maternity Allowance, Parenting Payment, Family Tax Payment, Health Care Cards, Maintenance enquiries, Double Orphan Pension Child Care Assistance Tel: 13 1524.

Enquiries in languages other than English Tel: 13 1202.
Youth & Student Services Tel: 13 2490.

For services including Youth Allowances:

Austudy Tel: 13 2490.

Assistance for Isolated Children Tel: 13 2318.

Centrelink Career Information. Information on Careers and further study Sydney Level 1, 477 Pitt St. Tel: 2000 (02) 9209 1650.

Enquiries by telephone for people with hearing & speech difficulties Freecall 1800 810 586.

Customer Relations Freecall 1800 050 004.
For Customer Service Feedback, Compliments, Comment:

Centrelink Employer Hotline 13 1158.
Fax 13 2115.
A service for employers for assistance with completing forms and general information on centre services and programs.

Centrelink International Services 1 Tel: 3 1673.
Includes assistance to claim pensions from Austria, Cyprus, Denmark, Ireland, Italy, Malta, Netherlands, Spain and The United Kingdom.

Centrelink Youth & Student Services Locations.
Refer to Centrelink Office Locations.

## CENTRELINK OFFICES

To make an appointment for any office in Australia, telephone Centrelink on 13 1021.

### New South Wales

Ashfield 320 Liverpool Rd
Auburn 3 Mary St
Bankstown 44 Raymond St
Baulkham Hills 7 Seven Hills Rd
Blacktown 38 Prince St
Bondi Junction 6 Carousel Shoprig Cntr 520 Oxford
Cabramatta 251–257 Cabramatta Rd

Camden 16–22 Murray St
Campbelltown 63 Queen St
Campsie 19 Anglo Rd
Caringbah 15–21 President Ave
Chatswood 56 Archer St
Darlinghurst 137 Crown St
Fairfield 29–33 Barbara St
Hornsby 117 Pacific Hwy
Hurstville 9 Crofts Ave
Ingleburn 68 Oxford Rd
Lakemba–Lakemba St(Cnr Croydon St)
Leichhardt 23 Balmain Rd
Liverpool 171 Bigge St
Liverpool Family Service Centre 278 Macquarie St
Maroubra 138 Maroubra Rd
Marrickville R73 Illawarra Rd
Merrylands 207 Pitt St
Mt Druitt  3 Mount St
Northern Beaches 660 Pittwater Rd
Nowra 61–63 North St
Paramatta Commonwealth Offices 2 Macquarie St
Penrith 81 Henry St
Redfern  George St(Crir Redfern St)
Revesby 1 Macarthur Ave.
Rockdale 75 Railway St
Ryde 19 Deviin St
Shellharbour Lamerton House, Shellharbour Centre
Springwood Shop 4, 107 Macquarie Rd
St Marys 47 Phillip St
Strathfield 2nd Floor Strathfield Plaza
Sutherland 30 Eton St
Windsor 309 George St
Centrelink Area Support Office
East Coast (Sydney)
Sydney 477 Pitt St 2000 (02) 9244 6000
Hunter
Charlestown 331 Charlestown Rd 2290 (02) 4974 3400
East Coast
Wollongong 43 Burelli St (02) 9244 6000
South Metropolitan
Liverpool George St (Cnr Moore St) 2170 (02) 9203 8400

South West
Queanbeyan 7 Morriset St 2620 (02) 6200 5757
West
Parramatta 2 Macquarie St 2150 (02) 9865 3600
Public Relations Enquiries Only (02) 9244 6444
Media Enquiries Only (02) 9244 6455

## Victoria

Ararat 64 High St
Bairnsdale 101 Nicholson St
Ballarat 1121 Albert St
Bendigo 231–235 Lyttleton Tce (Cnr St Andrews Ave)
Box Hill 3–13 Harrow St
Broadmeadows 16–22 Pearcedale Pde
Camberwell 1 Railwpy Pde
Cheltenham 1242 Nepean Hwy
Colac 55 Dennis St
Corio 1st Flr, Corio Village, Bacchus Marsh Rd
Cranboume 79 Codrington St
Dandenong 27–29 Robinson St
Darebin 273 High St Preston
Echuca 26 Percy St
Epping 713 High St
Essendon 333 Keilor Rd Essendon North
Ferntree Gully Shop 1, 1174 Burwood Hwy
Fitzroy 62–70 Johnston St
Footscray 11 Leeds St
Fountain Gate 42 Magid Drv
Frankston Davey St (Cnr Young St)
Geelong 129 Myers St (Pensions & Families)
Geelong 170 Little Malop St (Employment Services)
Glen Waverley 7 Bogong Ave
Greensborough 9–13 Flintoff St
Hamilton 86 French St
Heidelberg 21 Yarra St
Horsham Darlot St (Cnr Mclachlan St.)
Knox LA 2, Knox District Centre 2 Capital City Blv
Lilydale Anderson St (Cnr Chapel St)
Maryborough 82 Alma St
Melton Smith St (Cnr Mckenzie St)

Mildura 158–164 Langtree Ave (Cnr Eleventh St)
Moreland 172–186 Moreland Rd
Mornington 332 Main St
Morwell Elgin St (Cnr Chapel St)
Newmarket 482–490 Racecourse Rd Flemington
Newport 433–439 Melbourne Rd
Oakleigh 20–22 Atherton Rd
Portland 36 Gawler St
Richmond 172–174 Bridge Rd
Ringwood 2–6 Bond St
Rosebud 921 Nepean Hwy
Sale 140–154 York St
Seymour Shop 3–4 The Mall
Shepparton 298 Maude St
South Melbourne 123–127 Cecil St
Springvale 324 Springvale Rd
St Albans 101–103 Main Rd (West)
Stawell 52 Main St
Sunbury 22 O'shanassy St
Sunshine 34 Devonshire Rd (Employment Services)
Sunshine 45 Dickson St (Pensions & Families)
Swan Hill 221–225 Beveridge St
Wangaratta Ovens St (Cnr Faithful St)
Warragul 4–24 Mason St
Wannambool Shop 6, 109 Lava St
Wembee 20 Synnot St
Windsor 255 High St Prahran

## Queensland

Annerley 471 Annerley Rd
Beaudesert Post Office Sq Brisbane St
Beenleigh 98 George St
Browns Plains 105 Browns Plains Rd
Capalaba 42 Redland Bay Rd
Chermside 18 Banfield St
Fortitude Valley 435 St Pauls Tce
Goodna 2 Smiths Rd
Inala 20 Wirraway Pde
Ipswich East St (Cnr South St)
Mitchelton 55 Osborne Rd

Mt Gravatt 96 Mt GravattCapalaba Rd
Nundah 1176 Sandgate Rd
Redcliffe 159 Sutton St
Stones Corner 479 Logan Rd
Strathpine 242 Gympie Rd
Toowong 17 Lissner St
Woodridge 6 Ewing Rd
Wynnum 63 Bay Tce

## ACT

Braddon 13 Lonsdale
Belconnen Level 1, Northpoint Plaza, Chandler St
Tuggeranong Four Seasons House, Anketell
St Tuggeranong Town Centre
Woden Nrma House, Corinna St
Queanbeyan 183 Crawford St

## South Australia

Adelaide 55 Currie St
Berri 5 Riverview Dri
Broken Hill 361–365 Argent St
Ceduna East Tce (Cnr Merghiny Drv)
Coober Pedy Lot 715 Hutchison St
EdwcA.rd,town 938 South Rd
Elizabeth 30 Philip Hwy
Enfield 494 Regency Rd
Gawler 23 High St
Glenelg 12 Durham St
Kadina 22–24 Taylor St
Kilkenny 8 Regency Rd
Marden 375 Payneham Rd
Modbury 116 Reservoir Rd
Mount Barker 2 Cameron St
Mount Gambier 5 Percy St
Murray Bridge 8–12 Bridge St
Noarlunga Centre Ramsay Walk
Norwood 203 The Parade
Parkside 257 Fullarton Rd
Port Adelaide Dale St (Cnr Robe St)

Port Augusta 99 Commercial Rd
Port Lincoln 85–89 Tasman Tce
Port Pirie 99 1Ellen St
Salisbury 30 Gawler St
Torrensville 132 Henley Beach Rd
Victor Harbor Shops 15–18 Torrens St
Whyalla 169 Nicolsorl Ave
Centrelink Area Support Office
Adelaide 191 Pulteney St 5000 (08) 8306 2100

## Western Australia

Cannington 13 Leila St
Fremantle 7 Pakenham St
Gosnells 88 Lissiman St
Inaloo 384 Scarborough Beach Rd
Joondalup 68 Reid Prm
Kwinana Meares Ave (Cnr Chisham Ave)
Mandurah 15 Mandurah Rd
Midland 18 Viveash Rd
Milligan St
Milligan St (Cnr Wellington St) Perth City
Mirrabooka 22 Chesterfield Rd
Morley 38 Rudloc Rd
Rockingham
Rockingham City Shopping Centre, Simpson Ave
Spearwood
Phoenix Park Shopping Centre, 2 Lancaster Rd
(Cnr Rockingham Rd)
Victoria Park 117 Shppperton Rd
Administration 200 St Geo Tce Perth 6000 (08) 9229 3000

## Northern Territory

Darwin 24 Knuckey St
Casuarina 50 LI3radshaw Tce
Palmerston Temple Tce (Cnr Maluka St)
Katherine Randazzo Arc
Alice Springs 62 Hartley St
Tennant Creek Patterson St
Nhulunbuy Endeavour Sq

Broome Weld St
Derby 329 Clarendon St
Kununurra Konkerberry Drv
Centrelink Area Support Office
Darwin 18 Litchfield St 0800

## Tasmania

Befierive 1 Bligh St, Rosny Park
Bridgewater 24 Greenpoint Road
Glenorchy 3 Terry St (Cnr Cooper St)
Hobart Plaza Level, 188 Collins St
Huonville 40a Main Road
Centrelink Area Support Office
8.30am 5.00pm
Area Administration (03) 6222 3403

## JOBSEARCH

The government provides an online job searching service that gives lists of vacancies by state and also offer opportunities for both employers and employees to state their requirements. In mid-2000 there were more than 40,000 vacancies advertised on the site. To view the JobSearch site look at: www.jobsearch.gov.au/

## DEPARTMENT OF EMPLOYMENT, WORKPLACE RELATIONS AND SMALL BUSINESS

Another government Web site that offer employment information is the one for the Department of Employment, Workplace Relations and Small Business, which can be found by looking at: www.dewrsb.gov.au/ This is linked to another government employment site, Job Network, which can be found at: www.jobnetwork.gov.au/

## AUSTRALIAN WORKPLACE

This is a Government website that has information on employment, workplace relations, government assistance, jobs, careers, training and wages. More information can be found on the website at www.workplace.gov.au/

# 7

## The General Recruitment Network

### EMPLOYMENT AGENCIES

Employment agencies proliferate in Australia, particularly for occupations such as secretarial and management. The following list includes a short selection of agencies in various states. For a more extensive list consult the *Yellow Pages* for the relevant state. This can either be done once you get to Australia or check in the nearest large city library in your area to see if they have any copies. Alternatively, look at their Web site at www.yellowpages.com.au/

### Australian Capital Teritory (ACT)

The One Umbrella Pty Ltd, 2 Bradfield St.,. Downer, ACT 2602. Tel (02) 6242 1964. Web site: www.oneumbrella.com.au. Knowledge Management Staff, Records Staff, Library Staff, Archivists, Employment Services.

Employment National, Shop 1, NorthPoint Plaza 8, Chandler St., Belconnen, ACT 2617. Tel (02) 6219 5008. Temporary Clerical, Office and Administration Staff.

Dunhill Management Services Group Pty Ltd, Level 9, 60 Marcus Clarke St., Canberra City, ACT 2601. Tel (02) 6248 7700. Recruitment, Temporary Staff, Executive Search, Human Resources, Personnel.

ANU Student Employment Service, Ellery Crs, Acton, ACT 2601. Tel (02) 6249 3674 General employment services.

Accountancy Appointments, Level 3, Canberra House, 40 Marcus Clarke St., Canberra City, ACT 2601. Tel (02) 6257 1010. Accountacy staff and those involved in all areas of the financial services.

Alactus Personnel Pty Ltd, Level 2, Perpetual Trustees Building, 10 Rudd Street, Canberra City, ACT 2601. Tel (02) 6257 8111. General Employment Services.

Drake, 10–12 Campion St Deakin ACT 2600. Tel (02) 6281 1022. General employment service specialising in executive and industrial staff.

## New South Wales

Metro Personnel, Level 6, Thakral House, 301 George St., Sydney, NSW 2000. Tel (02) 9299 5477. Web site: www.metropersonnel.com.au Administration Staff, Banking & Legal, Call Centre Staff, Customer Service, Data Entry, Executive PA's, Receptionists, Secretaries, Telemarketers, WP Operators.

Options Enterprises Employment and Training Services, Chatswood, NSW 2067. Tel (02) 9412 3122. Web site: www.options.com.au Traineeships, Outplacement, Job Network Services, Recruitment, Training.

The One Umbrella Pty Ltd, Level 9, 162 Goulburn St., Surry Hills, NSW 2010. Tel (02) 9263 0000. Web site: www.oneumbrella.com.au Knowledge Management Staff, Records Staff, Library Staff, Archivists, Employment Services.

Library Locums, Level 9, 162 Goulburn St., Surry Hills, NSW 2010. Tel (02) 9263 0063. Web site: www.oneumbrella.com.au Researchers, Records Staff Recruitment, Library Staff Recruitment, Employment Services, Filers, Cataloguers, Knowledge Management Staff, Researchers, Library Information Staff, Knowledge Management Staff.

Service Industry Advisory Group, Sydney, NSW 2000. Tel 1800 65 6844. Web site: www.siag.com.au Payroll, Employment Law, Industrial Relations Products, Human Resource, Recruitment.

Interlogic Placements, Level 3, 121 Walker St., North Sydney, NSW 2060. Tel (02) 9922 2711. Web site: www.interlogic.com.au Finance, Telecommunications, Manufacturing, Sales, Electronics.

Jobworx Level 5, 6 O'Connell St., Sydney, NSW 2000. Tel (02) 9235 3555. Web site: www.jobworx.com.au IT Specialists, Permanent Recruitment, Internet Employment, Web Focused Recruitment, Contract Recruitment.

Michelle Adonis Consulting, Level 5, 280 George Street, Sydney, NSW 2000. Tel (02) 9233 7444. Web site: www.m-a-c.com.au. Accounting, Banking & Financial Services, Customer Service/Call Centres, Administrative Support, Sales & Marketing.

Greythorn Pty Ltd, Level 7, 50 Market St., Sydney, NSW 2000. Tel (02) 9249 8000. Web site: www.greythorn.com.au Web Developers, PC Support, Network Engineers, Programmers, IT Recruitment.

Computer 2000, 100 Walker St., North Sydney NSW 2060. Tel (02) 9964 0411. Web site: www.comp2000.com.au. IT placements.

Hallis, Level 20, 264–278 George Street, Sydney, NSW 2000. Tel (02) 9241 3966. Web site: http://hallis.com.au Research, Call Centre, Assessment Centre, Surveys, Recruitment.

## Queensland

Data 3 IT Careers and Contracts, 165 Moggill Rd., Taringa, QLD 4068. Tel (07) 3371 8088. Web site: www.data3.com.au/itcc IT placements, Temporary Assignments, Permanent Recruitment, Outsourcing Solutions, Contracting Services.

Catalyst Recruitment, Unit 4, 172 Evans Rd., Salisbury, QLD 4107. Tel 13 3301. Web site: www.catalystrecruitment.com.au Permanent Recruitment, Call Centre, Temporary Recruitment, Training, Telemarketing.

IPA Personnel, Suite 7, Level 7, 141 Queen St., Brisbane, QLD 4000. Tel (07) 3223 3500 (office throughout Australia too) Web site: www.ipagroup.com.au Temporary Recruitment Services, Permanent Recruitment Services, Assessment Centre Recruitment Services, Unbundled Recruitment Services, Executive Search.

Hallis, Ambrosia House, 4 Gardiner Cl., Milton, QLD 4064. Tel (07) 3369 1511. Web site: www.hallis.com.au. Senior and Executive, Sales and Call Centre, Admin and Support., Electronic and Internet, Office Support, Call Centre and Sales, Managed Workforces.

Axis HR, Level 15, 80 Albert St., Brisbane, QLD 4000. Tel (07) 3221 1442. Web site: www.axishr.com.au Accounting, Legal, Finance, Insurance.

Law Staff, Level 15, 80 Albert St., Brisbane, QLD 4000. Tel (07) 3221 1229. Web site: www.axishr.com.au Staff Solicitors, In-House Lawyers, Articled Clerks, Paralegals, Legal Secretaries, Legal Accounts Persons, Legal WP Operators, Outdoor Clerks.

Employment North Ltd, 41189 Musgrave St., North Rockhampton, QLD 4701. Tel 1800 24 8351. General employment services.

Jobs Australia, 104 Munns Drive, Woorabinda, QLD 4702. Tel (07) 4935 0257. General employment services.

Yulla Muna Employment Services, 6 East St., Rockhampton, QLD 4702. Tel (07) 4922 5549. General employment services.

## South Australia

IPA Personnel, 18–20 Grenfell Street, Adelaide, SA 5000. Tel (08) 8210 0600. Web site: www.ipagroup.com.au Temporary Recruitment Services, Permanent Recruitment Services, Assessment Centre Recruitment Services, Unbundled Recruitment Services, Executive Search.

Select Staff Pty Ltd, Level 4/12 Pirie St., Adelaide, SA 5000. Tel (08) 8468 8000. Web site: www.selectstaff.com.au Labour Hire, Office Support, Marketing, Trades, Sales.

Speakman, Stillwell & Associates Pty Ltd, 12 Pirie St., Adelaide, SA 5000. Tel (08) 8461 4444. Web site: www.speakmans.com.au Management Consultants, Executive Search Selection, Human Resource, Organisation Development.

Mission Employment South Australia, 49 Flinders St., Adelaide, SA 5000. Tel 1300 65 0012. Web site: www.mission.com.au Community Support Program, JPET, New Enterprise Incentive Scheme, NEIS, Job Placement.

Quality Staff Pty Ltd, Office F, North Adelaide Village, Archer St., North Adelaide SA 5006. Tel (08) 8367 0366. Engineering, Construction, Recruitment, Industrial.

Boss Personnel, 9/69 Burbridge Road, Hilton, SA 5033. Tel (08) 8352 2888. Web site: www.bosspersonnel.com.au All Trades, Transport, Executive, Process, Clerical, Technology, Production, Security, Management.

Reliance Staff Bureau, 5 Leigh St., Adelaide SA 5000. Tel (08) 8212 3866. Printing and copying staff.

Secretaire Recruitment and Training Pty Ltd, Ground Floor, 50 Hindmarsh Square, Adelaide, SA 5000. Tel (08) 8223 5900. Office administration.

Dial an Angel Pty Ltd, Angel House, 78 Melbourne St., North Adelaide, SA 5006. Tel (08) 8267 3700. General employment service.

## Victoria

CDS Personnel, Suite 6, 15–17 Pakington St., St. Kilda, VIC 3182. Tel (03) 9593 9555. Web site: www.cdspersonnel.com.au Personnel consultants, engineering, contract, drafting.

Catalyst Recruitment, 421–437 Grieve Pde., Altona North, VIC 3025. Tel 13 3301. Web site: www.catalystrecruitment.com.au Permanent Recruitment, Call Centre, Temporary Recruitment, Training, Telemarketing.

IPA Personnel, Level 15, 440 Collins St., Melbourne, VIC 3000. Tel (03) 9252 2222. Web site: www.ipagroup.com.au Temporary Recruitment Services, Permanent Recruitment Services, Assessment Centre Recruitment Services, Unbundled Recruitment Services, Executive Search.

Skilled Engineering Limited, 850 Whitehorse Road, Box Hill, VIC 3128. Tel (03) 9924 2424. Web site. www.skilled.com. au Office, trades, warehousing, hospitality, professionals.

DLA Consulting, Level 1, 114 William St., Melbourne, VIC 3000. Tel (03) 9670 4244.

Human Edge Recruitment, Level 1, 36–38 Clarke St., South Melbourne, VIC 3205. Tel (03) 9686 6369. Web site: www.dlaconsulting.com.au Training, recruitment, HR management.

Library Locums, 63 Stead St., South Melbourne, VIC 3205. Tel (03) 9645 0344. The One Umbrella Pty Ltd, Level 9, 162 Goulburn St., Surry Hills, NSW 2010. Tel (02) 9263 0000. Web site: www.oneumbrella.com.au. Knowledge Management Staff, Records Staff, Library Staff, Archivists, Employment Services.

Service Industry Advisory Group Pty Ltd, Level 3, 450 St. Kilda Rd., Melbourne, VIC 3000. Tel 1800 65 6844. Web site: www.siag.com.au Payroll, Employment Law, Industrial Relations Products, Human Resource, Recruitment.

Hallis, Level 3, 60 Albert Road, South Melbourne, VIC 3205. Tel (03) 9696 2144/3555. Web site: www.hallis.com.au Senior & Executive, Sales and Call Centre, Admin and Support, Electronic and Internet, Office Support, Call Centre and Sales, Managed Workforces.

DFP Recruitment Services, Level 8, 379 Collins St., Melbourne, VIC 3000. Tel (03) 9620 9900. Web site: www.dfarmer.com.au Management, sales, office, call centre.

Riddells Staffing, 128 Exhibition St., Melbourne, VIC 3000. Tel (03) 9650 1044. Web site: www.riddells.com.au General recruitment.

## Western Australia

Sure Personnel Pty Ltd, 246 Stirling St., Perth, WA 6000. Tel (08) 9328 7400. General recruitment.

Olympia Business School, 177a St. Georges Tce., Perth, WA 6000. Tel (08) 9321 9899. Web site: www.olympia.wa.edu.au General recruitment.

Execom Resources, Upper Plaza, QV1 Building, 250 St. Georges Tce., Perth, WA 6000. Tel (08) 9429 6040. Web site: www.execomre sources.com.au Contract, payroll, senior management, engineering, IT.

Office Angels, MHP Recruitment Group, Level 6, East Point Plaza, 233

Adelaide Tee., Perth, WA 6000. Tel (08) 9421 1522. Web site: www.officeangels.com.au Executive, permanent and temporary office staff.

David Christie & Associates Pty Ltd, Suite 4, 20 Altona St., West Perth, WA 6005. Tel, (08) 9321 1574. Web site: www.davidchristie.com.au IT and executives.

Talent International Pty Ltd, Level 8, 37 Georges Tce., Perth, WA 6000. Tel (08) 92213300. Web site: www.talent–int.com.au Computing and IT.

Anson, 17 Ord St., West Perth, WA 6005. Tel (08) 93210000. Web site: www.anson.com.au Accounting, sales, financial, marketing.

Choice Personnel Group, 262 St. Georges Tce., Perth, WA 6000. Tel (08) 9321 2011. Web site: www.choice.net.au Home help, nursing, occupational health.

Meditemp, 262 St. Georges Tce., Perth, WA 6000. Tel (08) 93212066. (See Choice Personnel Group above)

## NEWSPAPERS

With at least two daily newspapers in most major Australian cities and up to six in Sydney there is no shortage of newsprint to peruse in the Jobs Vacant Sections. Most of the major newspapers carry extensive employment sections, covering all sectors of the employment market, from business executives to deck-hands on prawn trawlers.

The main big city newspapers are:

*The Sydney Morning Herald*, 235 Jones Street, Broadway, Sydney 2007. Tel: 02 9282 2822.
*The Melbourne Age*, 250 Spencer Street, Melbourne. Tel: 03 9601 2676.
*The Adelaide Advertiser*, 121 King William Street, Adelaide. Tel: 08 8218 9760.
*The Brisbane Courier-Mail*, Campbell Street, Bowen Hills, Brisbane. Tel: 07 3252 6011.
*The West Australian*, 219 St. George's Terrace, Perth. Tel: 09 482 3111.

## Abbreviations in job advertisements

The following is a list of the abbreviations, and their meanings, which appear most frequently in newspaper job advertisements in Australia.

| | | | |
|---|---|---|---|
| acc. | according to | cas. | casual |
| dir | director | gen. | general |
| adm | administrative | co. | company |
| dept . | department | hrs. | hours |
| an. lve. | annual leave | coll. | college |
| D/L | Driving Licence | immed. | immediate |
| app. | applicant | comm. | commensurate with |
| D.O.B. | Date of Birth | | interview |
| appshp. | apprenticeship | int. | interview |
| DP | Data Processing | conds. | conditions |
| AP | accounts payable | K (or M) | thousand |
| A/R | accounts received | CV | Curriculum Vitae |
| EDP | electronic data processing | knwl | knowledge |
| apt. | appointment | deg. | degree |
| em. | employer/ment | maj. | major |
| asst. | assistant | max. | maximum |
| ess. | essential | ref/s | reference/s |
| av. | average | metro. | metropolitan |
| exc. | excluding | remun. | remuneration |
| avail. | available | M/F | male/female |
| exec. | executive | rep. | representative |
| Awd | Award | mfr. | manufacturer |
| exp. | experience | reqd | required |
| bgnr. | beginner | mgmt | management |
| F/C | full charge | S. A. E. | Stamped Addressed |
| bfts. | benefits | | Envelope |
| fnl. | financial | min. | minimum |
| bus. | business | mktg | marketing |
| F/Pd | fee paid | sal. | salary |
| F/T | full-time | mth. | month |
| P/T | part-time | sec. | secretary |
| sten. | stenographer | urg. | urgent |
| norm. | normal | ph. | phone |
| svc. | service | vac/y | vacant/vacancy |
| occ. | occupation | P.O.B. | post office box |
| tech. | technical | wk. | week/work |
| opp. | opportunity | pref. | preferred |
| temp. | temporary | wkly. | weekly |
| O/T | overtime | prev. | previous |
| trng. | training | ww.p.m. | words per minute |
| p. a. | per annum | quals. | qualifications |
| trvl. | travel | recept. | receptionist |
| pd. | paid | R & D | research and |
| typg | typing | | development |
| perm. | permanent | yrs | years |

**Is this you?**

Accountant

Actuary

Farm worker

Radio/TV announcer

Architect

Designer

Fashion illustrator

Air traffic controller

Airline steward/ess

Beauty therapist

Builder

Cabinet-maker

Carpenter

Painter/decorator

Nursery nurse

Chiropractor

Computer programmer

Data processor

Community worker

Chef

Performing artist

Dentist

Economist

Film technician

Television researcher

Forestry worker

Geologist

Graphic designer

Hairdresser

Health worker

Horticulturist

Caterer

Insurance officer

Journalist

Lawyer

Locksmith

Doctor

Metalworker

Miner

Editor

Technical writer

Oil driller

Optician

Photographer

Physiotherapist

Printer

Prison officer

Public service officer

Surveyor

Leisure manager

Researcher

Teacher

Advertising agent

Ambulance officer

Artist

Photographer

Bank officer

Bricklayer

Plumber

Childminder

Systems analyst

Conservationist

Defence worker

Engineer

Food technologist

Glazier

Health officer

Hotelier

Jeweller

Librarian

Nurse

Musician

Therapist

Pharmacist

Police officer

Psychologist

Ranger

Retailer

Australia offers a huge variety of employment opportunities.

# 8

## Careers and Professions

There are a wide variety of careers available in Australia. These can either be entered by people who have gained relevant qualifications or experience in Britain, or training can be undertaken in Australia. In some cases, skills and qualifications will need to be assessed before you can take up an equivalent post in Australia. This will be dealt with in the following chapter. Addresses for the universities and further education establishments mentioned here are given in the chapter on Training.

The wages mentioned here should be used as a guide only, as more and more wage settlements are now being decided by performance.

### ACCOUNTING

This covers a wide range of disciplines including accounting staff, accountant assistant, cost accountant, senior accounting executive, chief accountant, financial executive, research, Organisation and Methods, internal auditor, evaluator of projects and programs, and security analyst.

*Qualification required:* Degree
*Where to study:* Most major universities and Technical and Further Education (TAFE) colleges in all states.
*Current workforce:* 100,000+.
*Future prospects:* Very good.
*Starting wage:* Various depending on the type of accounting.
*Further information:* The National Institute of Accountants, GPO Box 1128J, Melbourne, Victoria 3001.

### ACTUARY

An expert in the theory and practice of statistics. They are called upon to deal with a wide range of statistical problems arising in insurance, superannuation funds, health insurance and a variety of other areas of finance. Most actuaries are employed by insurance companies or in private consultancies.

*Qualification required:* Degree.

*Where to study:* Australian University, Bond University, Queensland University of Technology, Macquarie University, University of Melbourne.

*Current workforce:* 2,000+.

*Future prospects:* Good.

*Starting wage:* $690+.

*Wage after three years:* $900+.

*Further information:* The Institute of Actuaries of Australia, Suite 1, 8th Floor, 49 Market Street, Sydney. Tel: 02 264 2411.


## ADVERTISING

### Account Manager

This is an advertising agency's representative to the client. He or she will be responsible for the overall advertising and marketing campaign of a specific product or image.

*Qualification required:* Degree

*Where to study:* Bond University, Charles Sturt University, Deakin University, Edith Cowan University, Queensland University of Technology, Victoria University of Technology — RMIT, University College of Central Queensland, University of New England, University of Western Sydney, Macleay College, Sydney. Also TAFE colleges in all states.

*Current workforce:* 2,500+.

*Future prospects:* Good.

*Starting wage:* $600+.

*Wage after three years:* $850+.

*Further information:* The Advertising Federation of Australia Ltd, 140 Arthur Street, North Sydney, NSW 2060.


### Copywriter

The person who writes the scripts for radio, television and printed advertisements.

*Qualification required:* Degree.

*Where to study:* As above.

*Current workforce:* 800+.

*Future prospects:* Good.

*Starting wage:* $625+.

*Wage after three years:* $850+.
*Further information:* As above.


## AGRICULTURE AND FARM MANAGEMENT

Farming in Australia has become a tough occupation in recent years and today's farmers need to be managers, book-keepers, mechanics, veterinarians, agronomists and accountants.

Farm management is not just the process of running a farm, but organising land, labour and capital. However, unless you come from a farming family you will have to start near the bottom of the rung if you want to break into farming. The most common way to do this is as a farm hand or a dairy farm worker. This involves long hours and hard work but it can lead to a career in farm management:

*Current workforce:* 250,000+.
*Future prospects:* Numbers are likely to decline due to the recession in the farming industry.
*Starting wage:* $400+.
*Wage after three years:* $660+.
*Further information:* Victorian Farmers Federation, 240 Collins Street, Melbourne 3000. Tel: 03 650 9261. NSW Rural Training Committee, GPO Box 1068, Sydney 2001. United Farmers and Stockowners Association, 126 South Terrace, Adelaide 5000.


## AMBULANCE SERVICE

### Ambulance officer
Undertake similar work to ambulance officers in Britain; attending home, work and car accidents. They are also likely to be called to incidents such as accidents in bush country or cliff rescues.


### Paramedic
Paramedics attend life-threatening emergencies and have to have at least three years' experience as an ambulance officer and have passed all in-service training courses.


### Rescue Squad Officers
These officers are involved in getting people trapped in accidents to hospital. Three years' experience as an ambulance officer is required and comprehensive training is given.

## Co-ordinators

Co-ordinators work in the centre where the emergency calls are received. They must have three years' experience as an ambulance officer and attend an eight week in-service training course.

*Qualifications:* In-service training and part-time TAFE courses.
*Current workforce:* 6,000.
*Future prospects:* Growth expected.
*Starting wage:* $460+.
*Wage after three years:* $650+.
*Further information:* Career Reference Centres, Careers Advisers, Health Commission, in the relevant state.

## ANNOUNCER

Can be news readers, disc jockeys or commentators for television or radio. A clear voice and a calm temperament are vital qualities and most announcers begin their careers on country radio stations.

*Where to study:* The Australian Film, Television and Radio School, PO Box 126, North Ryde, NSW.
*Current workforce:* 2,000+.
*Future prospects:* Hard to break in to but industry growth is expected.
*Starting wage:* $575+.
*Wage after three years:* $700+.
*Further information:* The Australian Broadcasting Corporation, GPO Box 9994, Sydney 2001.

## ARCHITECT

Openings for qualified architects but also numerous opportunities for training in Australia.

*Qualification:* Degree.
*Where to study:* Universities of Adelaide, Canberra, Melbourne, New South Wales, Newcastle, Queensland, South Australia, Tasmania and Curtain and Deakin Universities.
*Current workforce:* 15,000.
*Future prospects:* Reasonable growth but has been hit by the recession.
*Starting wage:* $525+.
*Wage after three years:* $650+.

*Further information:* Royal Institute of Architects, NSW Chapter, 3 Manning Street, Potts Point, NSW.

## ART AND DESIGN

Covering commercial artists, community artworkers, community arts officers, graphic designers, textile and fashion designers, industrial designers, illustrators, advertising layout artists, photographers, window dressers and sculptors.

*Where to train:* As above, plus Ballarat University College, Charles Sturt University, Riverina, Griffith University, La Trobe University College of Northern Victoria, Monash University, Swinburne Institute of Technology, School of Visual Art, East Sydney, The KVB College of Visual Communication and Billy Blue School of Art.

*Current workforce:* 50,000.

*Future prospects:* Good — self-employment is a serious option for many people in art and design.

*Starting wage:* $525+.

*Wage after three years:* $650+.

*Further information:* School of Art and Design, East Sydney Technical College, Forbes Street, Darlinghurst, NSW. The Crafts Council of Australia, 35 George Street, The Rocks, Sydney. The National Association for the Visual Arts, 1/245 Chalmers Street, Redfern.

## AIR TRAFFIC SERVICES

### Air Traffic Controllers

Responsible for all aircraft movements inside and outside controlled airspace.

*Qualifications:* Specialist training courses.

Where to study: University of Tasmania, Civil Aviation Authority — twelve month on-the-job training for former pilots and defence air traffic controllers.

*Current workforce:* 3,900.

*Future prospects:* Average.

*Starting wage:* $700.

*Wage after three years:* $770.

*Further information:* Civil Aviation Authority, GPO Box 367, Canberra 2601.

Defence Force Recruiting Centre, 323 Castlereagh Street, Sydney 2000.

## Flight attendants

Generally they must be between 1.6m and 1.83m in height, in good health and preferably have previous experience of the catering industry and knowledge of a foreign language.

*Qualifications:* Special airline training courses.
*Where to study:* Individual airlines provide their own training.
*Current workforce:* 10,000.
*Future prospects:* Good.
*Starting wage:* $550.
*Wage after three years:* $650.
*Further information:* Qantas Airways Limited, Jamison Street, Sydney 2000.
Australian Airlines, Hunter and Philip Streets, Sydney 2000.
East-West Airlines, Level 3, 431 Glebe Point Road, Glebe 2037.
Ansett Airlines and Air NSW, Oxford Square, Oxford and Riley Streets, Sydney 2000.

## BANK OFFICER

The way in for most people to the banking trade. This can lead to several areas of banking including administration, secretarial, accountancy, auditing, international banking and portfolio management.

*Qualifications:* A minimum of four years' secondary schooling. Some banks also operate entrance examinations. In-house training is given for successful applicants. Graduates are greatly in demand by banks and they are usually thought of as head office and senior management material.
*Where to study:* Australian Catholic University (Mackillop Campus, North Sydney) offers a degree course in Banking and Finance.
*Current workforce:* Teller: 56,000+. Bank branch managers: 14,000+. Bank accountants: 75,000+.
*Future prospects:* Good.
*Starting wage:* $400+ (Tellers).
*Wage after three years:* $500+ (Tellers).
*Further information:* All bank branch managers. Also the Australian Bank Employees Union, PO Box 435, Milsons Point 2061.

## BEAUTY THERAPY

People over the age of 21 years old are preferred for most beauty salons. Experience in cosmetic sales or hairdressing are desirable as a basic grounding in the beauty business. Training in beauty therapy is regulated by the Advanced Association of Beauty Therapists (AABTh).

*Training:* Mostly done in salons or in specialised schools.
*Where to study:* Technical and Further Education (TAFE) colleges throughout Australia.
*Current workforce:* 7,500+.
*Future prospects:* Good.
*Starting wage:* $400+.
*Wage after three years:* $480+.
*Further information:* Advanced Association of Beauty Therapists, PO Box 2885, GPO Sydney 2001.

## BUILDING TRADES

The building trade has been slow to recover from the recession but it is on the mend and there are still possibilities for casual employment or a career in building.

### Bricklayer
*Training:* Apprenticeship.
*Where to study:* TAFE and on-the-job training.
*Current workforce:* 39,000.
*Future prospects:* Improving.
*Starting wage:* $560+.
*Wage after three years:* $600+.

### Cabinet-maker
*Training:* Apprenticeship.
*Where to study:* TAFE and on-the-job training.
*Current workforce:* 30,000.
*Future prospects:* Some small growth expected.
*Starting wage:* $460+.
*Wage after three years:* $600+.

### Carpenter/Joiner
*Training:* Apprenticeship.
*Where to study:* TAFE and on-the-job training.
*Current workforce:* 110,000+.
*Future prospects:* Average.
*Starting wage:* $550+.
*Wage after three years:* $580+.

## Plumber
*Training:* Apprenticeship.
*Where to study:* TAFE and on-the-job training.
*Current workforce:* 50,000+.
*Future prospects:* Improving.
*Starting wage:* $570+.
*Wage after three years:* $600+.

## Plasterer
*Training:* Apprenticeship.
*Where to study:* TAFE and on-the-job training.
*Current workforce:* 20,000+.
*Future prospects:* Some growth expected.
*Starting wage:* $550+.
*Wage after three years:* $575+.

## Painter and decorator
*Training:* Apprenticeship.
*Where to study:* TAFE and on-the-job training.
*Current workforce:* 40,000+.
*Future prospects:* Average.
*Starting wage:* $470+.
*Wage after three years:* $560+.

## Building technician
This is a combination of a tradesperson and the duties of a professional builder.
*Training:* Apprenticeship and Associate Diploma Courses.
*Where to study:* TAFE and on-the-job training.
*Current workforce:* 27,000+.
*Future prospects:* Little growth expected.
*Starting wage:* $550+.
*Wage after three years:* $670+.

## Professional builder
These are people, generally with a building related degree, who work on large building projects. They are involved in technological, managerial and economic decisions.

*Training:* Apprenticeship and Associate Diploma, or Degree, or

Graduate Diploma.

*Where to study:* TAFE, on-the-job training and at universities through-out Australia.

*Current workforce:* 30,000+.

*Future prospects:* Good.

*Starting wage:* $575+.

*Wage after three years:* $640+.

Further information for all aspects of the building trade:

- Building Careers Information Centre, 6-12 Atchison Street, St Leonard NSW 2065. Postal address: Box 508, St Leonard.

- The Building Workers Industrial Union, 490 Kent Street, Sydney, NSW 2000.

- The Master Builders Association, 52 Parrish Road, Forest Lodge, NSW 2037.

- TAFE Information Centre, Railway Square, Broadway, NSW 2007.

## CHILD CARE

Most child care workers work in child care centres and kindergartens, many of them run by organisations including the Kindergarten Union of NSW, Sydney Day Nursery and the Nursery Schools Association.

*Qualifications:* Degree, diploma or certificate courses.

*Where to study:* Universities of Melbourne, South Australia, Western Australia and Western Sydney, Queensland University of Technology, Northern Territory University, Charles Sturt University, Edith Cowan University, Hedland College, Macquarie University and TAFE colleges.

*Current workforce:* 90,000.

*Future prospects:* Good.

*Starting wage:* Child care worker: $300+. Child care co-ordinator: $580.

*Wage after three years:* Child care worker: $385. Child care co-ordinator: $660.

## CHIROPRACTOR

There are several openings for chiropractors to set up their own practices in Australia. There are also opportunities in clinics, teaching and research.

*Qualifications:* Degree.
*Where to study:* Macquarie University, Philip Institute of Technology.
*Current workforce:* 1400+.
*Future prospects:* Average.
*Starting wage:* $660+.
*Wage after three years:* $870+.
*Further information:* Philip Institute of Technology, Plenty Road, Bundoora, Victoria 3083.
The Australian Chiropractics Association in individual states.

## COMPUTING

This is an area in which jobs and wages depend greatly on experience and qualifications. The wages quoted here are less than experienced staff can expect.

### Systems Analysts/Programmers
*Qualifications:* An accountancy qualification or tertiary training in commerce, economics, computer science, science or engineering is recommended.
*Where to study:* Most Australian universities and TAFE colleges offer relevant courses.
*Current workforce:* 100,000+.
*Future prospects:* Good.
*Starting wage:* $750+.
*Wage after three years:* $900+.
*Further information:* The Australian Computer Society, 66 King Street, Sydney, NSW 2000.

### Computer operators/Word processing operators/Data preparation operators
*Training:* TAFE and private college courses.
*Where to study:* As above.
*Current workforce:* 130,000+.
*Future prospects:* Good.
*Starting wage:* $400+.

*Wage after three years:* $550+.
*Further information:* As above and Metropolitan Business College, 74 Wentworth Avenue, Sydney, NSW 2010.

## COMMUNITY ARTS

A relatively new career in which artists are employed to design and paint murals, plan and build playgrounds, develop community festivals, write and perform music for community groups and research and write local histories. The people who organise these activities are Community Arts Officers. Most of these posts are at least partly subsidised by the Australia Council.

*Qualifications:* Degree, diploma or associate diploma.
*Where to study:* Arts, humanities or social science qualifications at universities around Australia.
*Current workforce:* 250+.
*Future prospects:* Good.
*Starting wage:* $650+.
*Wage after three years:* $800+.
*Further information:* Special Project Officer (Community Arts Officers), Community Development Unit, Australia Council, Lawson Street, Redfern, NSW 2060. NSW Community Arts Association, Box 44, Trades Hall, Goulburn Street, Sydney, NSW 2000.

## CONSERVATOR/ART RESTORER

*Qualifications:* Degree.
*Where to study:* University of Canberra.
*Current workforce:* 900+.
*Future prospects:* Good.
*Further information:* University of Canberra, PO Box 1, Belconnen, ACT 2616.

## COOK/CHEF

This is another area which could be particularly fruitful for migrants — European chefs and cooks are highly thought of and there are openings within all areas of the catering industry for qualified personnel. Training can also be undertaken on arrival in the country.

*Training:* Apprenticeship (usually four years) and on-the-job training.
*Where to study:* TAFE colleges in all states.
*Current workforce:* 70,000.
*Future prospects:* Good.
*Starting wage:* $330+.
*Wage after three years:* $510+.
*Further information:* Federated Liquor and Allied Industries Union, 19 Argyle Street, Parramatta, NSW 2150. The Catering Institute of Australia, GPO Box 157, Sydney, NSW 2001. The Australian Hotels Association, 60 Clarence Street, Sydney NSW 2000. Restaurant and Catering Trades Association of NSW, 32 Buckingham Street, Surry Hills, NSW 2010.

## DANCE

Australia is becoming increasingly appreciative of the performing arts and dance is one area where talented people should be able to find work.

*Training:* Various, including degree, diploma and courses at private schools.
*Where to study:* Australian College of Physical Education, Victorian College of the Arts, The Australian Ballet School.
*Current workforce:* 900+.
*Future prospects:* Average — outstanding talent is the only way to ensure employment.
*Starting wage:* $450+.
*Wage after three years:* $620+.
*Further information:* The Australian Ballet School, 2 Kavanagh Street, South Melbourne, Victoria. Tel: 03 649 8600. Australian Association for Dance Education, PO Box 287, Jamison, ACT 2614.

## DEFENCE FORCES

There are currently just under 70,000 people in the Australian Defence Forces. To be eligible to join you must be an Australian citizen, or be eligible to become one, pass a medical, pass an aptitude test, have the required education qualifications, be within prescribed age limits and be prepared to serve anywhere. Almost every civilian post has a parallel in the Navy, Army and Airforce and every year the services need to enlist 6,000 new recruits. Training is offered in a wide range of skills.

The most common form of entry into the Defence Forces is through the **Defence Forces Academy** (applicants must usually be between 17 and 20 years of age), apprenticeships, or direct entrants from civilian careers.

*Further information:* Defence Forces Recruiting Centre, Central Square, 323 Castlereagh Street, NSW 2000, or enquiries can be sent to Director of Recruiting, Box XYZ in any state capital city.

## DENTISTRY

Similar to the dentistry business in Britain — dentists or prospective dentists are always in demand.

*Qualification:* Degree — a five year course within Australia.
*Where to study:* Universities of Melbourne, Queensland, Sydney, Adelaide and Western Australia.
*Current workforce:* 6,400+.
*Future prospects:* Good.
*Starting wage:* $950+.
*Wage after three years:* $1100+.
*Further information* (including dental assistants): Dean of the faculty of dentistry at the above universities. NSW Dental Assistants Association, Mail Box 47, Trades Hall, Goulburn Street, Sydney 2000.

## DRAFTING

Covers a variety of careers including architectural drafter, survey drafter and cartographic drafter.

*Qualifications:* Associate Diploma of Advanced Certificate courses.
*Where to study:* TAFE colleges in all states.
*Current workforce:* 27,000 covering all three categories.
*Future prospects:* Good.
*Starting wage:* $550+.
*Wage after three years:* $690+.
*Further information:* TAFE information centres.

## DRAMA

As in other parts of the world there are more people who want to be actors/actresses than there are openings in the profession. This inevitably leads to a large number of people in the drama profession being 'between jobs'.

*Training:* Degree, Diploma or Associate Diploma.
*Where to study:* The premier choice is the **National Institute of Dramatic Art** (NIDA). They offer three full-time diploma courses in Acting, Technical Production and Design and two full-time diploma courses in Theatre Crafts and a one year full-time diploma course in Directing. Applicants are accepted from all over the country and they also run courses covering other aspects of drama. Auditions for the Acting and Directing courses are held between November and December in all state capital cities. Various other courses are held at most Australian universities.
*Current workforce:* 2,200.
*Future prospects:* Average.
*Starting wage:* $480+.
*Wage after three years:* $575+.
*Further information:* National Institute of Dramatic Art, PO Box 1, Kensington, NSW 2033.

## ECONOMIST

Prospects for economists look very bright, particularly as they are no longer being blamed for the passing recession.

*Qualifications:* Degree.
*Where to study:* Most Australian universities.
*Current workforce:* 3,000.
*Future prospects:* Very good.
*+Starting wage:* $740.
*Wage after three years:* $990+.
*Further information:* Economics faculty at any university.

## ELECTRONIC ENGINEERING

A growing industry with opportunities in areas such as private industry and the consultancy, in hospitals, in radio and television and government departments.

*Qualification:* Degree.
*Where to study:* Most Australian universities.
*Current workforce:* 30,000+.
*Future prospects:* Good.
*Starting wage:* $660+.
*Wage after three years:* $850+.

### Electronic Engineering Technician

*Qualifications:* Associate Diploma or Advanced Certificate (usually two years). Also civilian traineeships with the Department of Commerce.
*Where to study:* TAFE colleges in all states.
*Current workforce:* 36,000+.
*Future prospects:* Good.
*Starting wage:* $600+.
*Wage after three years:* $700+.
*Further information:* Institution of Radio and Electronics Engineers, Australia Commercial Unit 3, 2 New McLean Street, Edgecliff, NSW.

### ENGINEERING

This covers several professions: professional engineering; civil engineering; electrical engineering; mechanical engineering; chemical engineering; maritime engineering; mining engineering; metallurgical engineering; agricultural engineering; aeronautical engineering; production engineering and industrial engineering.

Professional engineers are paid according to a nationally agreed pay award and they should hold a qualification which satisfies The Institute of Engineers.

*Qualification:* Degree.
*Where to study:* Most Australian universities.
*Current workforce:* 85,000.
*Future prospects:* Average – good.
*Starting wage:* $625+.
*Wage after three years:* $880+.
*Further information:* The Institute of Engineers, 118 Alfred Street, Milsons Point, NSW 2061.
The Association of Consulting Engineers Australia, 75 Miller Street, North Sydney, NSW 2060.

## FASHION DESIGNER

*Qualifications:* Degree, Diploma, Associate Diploma and Certificate courses.
*Where to study:* TAFE colleges, Victorian College of Technology, University of Tasmania, University of Technology, Sydney.
*Current workforce:* 2,000+.
*Future prospects:* Good.
*Starting wage:* $560+.
*Wage after three years:* $690+.
*Further information:* TAFE colleges in all states.

## FILM AND TELEVISION

An industry which employs people with a variety of skills: scriptwriter; producer; art director; production designer; director; sound recordist; director of photography; and editor.

The best way to break into the film and television industry is to apply to the Australian Film and Television School which is the national film, television and radio authority. The aim of the school is to maintain a continuing supply of skilled professionals for these industries. It does not give basic training for people with no experience. A three-year full-time degree course is offered as well as shorter courses, varying from three months to two years. Applicants are aged between 18 to 35 years and need to show a commitment to working in film and television.

*Further information:* The Australian Film and Television School, PO Box 126 North Ryde, NSW 2113. Tel: 02 805 6446. For an authoritative and readable careers guide see *Getting into Films & Television* by Robert Angell, a BAFTA Council Member (How To Books).

## FISHING

The creation of a 200-mile Australian fishing zone has led to greater possibilities for the use of fishing resources in the country. The onset of more deep sea fishing means that there is a greater use of modern technology in all sectors of the fishing industry. This now means that there are other careers available than those of fisherman/woman or skipper. These include fishing gear technologist, seafood marketing manager, fisheries biologist and fisheries inspector.

*Further information:* Australian Maritime College, PO Box 986, Launceston, Tasmania 7250. Tel: 003 26 6493.

## FOOD TECHNOLOGY

The hi-tech side of the food industry, this covers all aspects of preserving and processing of all foodstuffs.

*Qualifications:* Degree, Associate Diploma or Advanced Certificate.
*Where to study:* Universities of New South Wales, Newcastle, Queensland, Tasmania, Western Australia, and Australian Maritime College, and Ballarat University College.
*Current workforce:* 10,000+.
*Future prospects:* Good.
*Starting wage:* $575+.
*Wage after three years:* $750+.

## FORESTRY

The main areas covered are protection, management, silviculture (growing and tending of trees), wood technology and utilisation, and engineering.

*Qualifications:* Degree.
*Where to study:* Specific forestry courses at Australian National University, and universities of Melbourne and Queensland. Also agricultural courses at universities and colleges throughout the country.
*Current workforce:* 1,300.
*Future prospects:* Average.
*Starting wage:* $550.
*Wage after three years:* $700+.
*Further information:* Institute of Foresters of Australia, PO Box Q213, Queen Victoria Building, Sydney, NSW 2000.

## GARDENER/GREENKEEPER

*Training:* TAFE Certificate Courses, Apprenticeships and on-the-job training.
*Where to study:* TAFE colleges in all states.
*Current workforce:* 43,000.

*Future prospects:* Average.
*Starting wage:* $300+.
*Wage after three years:* $410+.
*Further information:* TAFE Information Centres.

## GEOLOGY

The demand for geologists varies according to the demands of the occasionally volatile mining industry. If you are in the right place at the right time there should be plenty of opportunities in the fields of petroleum exploration, mining and mineral extraction, underground water resources and engineering projects.

*Qualifications:* Degree or Diploma.
*Where to study:* Courses at universities in all states.
*Current workforce:* 6,000.
*Future prospects:* Good.
*Starting wage:* $680+.
*Wage after three years:* $750+.
*Further information:* Australian Institute of Geoscientists, Suite 10001, Challis House, 10 Martin Place, Sydney, NSW 2000. Tel: 02 231 4695.

## GLAZIERS/FLAT GLASS WORKERS

Most glaziers in Australia work for glass merchants. With some experience and capital it is possible to set up your own business after a few years.

*Training:* Apprenticeship.
*Where to study:* TAFE colleges in all states.
*Current workforce:* 6,600.
*Future prospects:* Good.
*Starting wage:* $300+.
*Wage after three years:* $525+.
*Further information:* NSW Glass Merchants Association, Private Bag 938, North Sydney 2060.

## GRAPHIC DESIGNER/COMMERCIAL ARTISTS

Work in the creation of advertisements for newspapers and magazines, promotional stationery, visual aids, book covers, television graphics, posters, pamphlets and postage stamps. They are usually hired by firms and organisations.

*Qualifications:* Degree, Diploma or Associate Diploma.
*Where to study:* Most main universities and the School of Visual Art, The KVB College of Visual Communication, Billy Blue School of Art, Australian College of Photography, Art and Communication.
*Current workforce:* 17,000.
*Future prospects:* Very good.
*Starting wage:* $600+.
*Wage after three years:* $750+.
*Further information:* The Design Institute of Australia in all states.

## HAIRDRESSING

There are opportunities for the trainee and also experienced hairdressers — particularly in the large cities. Australians in general take a great deal of interest in their appearance.

*Training:* Apprenticeship — a four year apprenticeship with a licensed hairdresser.
*Where to study:* TAFE colleges in all states. There are one year pre-employment courses which are followed by an apprenticeship of two and a half years with a licensed hairdresser.
*Current workforce:* 43,000.
*Future prospects:* Good.
*Starting wage:* $300+.
*Wage after three years:* $450+.
*Further information:* Australian Workers Union, 245 Chalmers Street, Redfern, NSW 2016.
Hairdressers Association, Suite 904, 9th Level, Aetna Life Tower, Hyde Park Square, Sydney, NSW 2000.

## HEALTH SURVEYOR/ENVIRONMENTAL HEALTH OFFICER

They ensure community services maintain good health standards. They are usually employed by municipal councils and government health departments.

*Qualifications:* Degree or Associate Diploma.
*Where to study:* Universities of Adelaide, Canberra, New England,

Wollongong, Western Sydney and Curtain University of Technology, Edith Cowan University, Griffith University and Queensland University of Technology. Also TAFE colleges in all states.
*Current workforce:* 5,000.
*Future prospects:* Good.
*Starting wage:* $550+.
*Wage after three years:* $700+.
*Further information:* The Australian Institute of Environmental Health, 22 Jarrett Street, Leichhardt, NSW.

## HOSPITAL AND HEALTH ADMINISTRATORS

Deal with the provision, management and evaluation of the health service. Most jobs are in hospital administration, Commonwealth, state and regional health services authorities, and private sector organisations.

*Qualifications:* Degree or Associate Diploma.
*Where to study:* Curtain University of Technology, La Trobe University, and universities of New England, New South Wales and South Australia.
*Current workforce:* 3,800.
*Future prospects:* Good.
*Starting wage:* $700.
*Wage after three years:* $900.
*Further information:* The Education Officer, Australian College of Health Service Administration, c/o Hornsby Hospital, Palmerston Road, Hornsby, NSW 2077.

## HOME ECONOMICS

A variety of possibilities involving testing recipes, preparing new products, advising on diet and testing for quality control. Opportunities exist with county councils, equipment and food manufacturers, government authorities, food producers and various food literature publishers.
*Qualifications:* Degree or Associate Diploma.
*Where to study:* Hawthorn Institute of Education, Queensland University of Technology, Victoria College of Technology and universities of Sydney, Tasmania and Western Australia.
*Future prospects:* Good.
*Further information:* Home Economics Association of NSW, GPO Box 2230, Sydney, NSW 2001.

## HORTICULTURE

Several careers are available in horticulture: professional horticulturist; nurseryman; landscape designer; and gardener.

*Qualifications:* Degree or Associate Diploma, TAFE Certificate Courses, Apprenticeships and on-the-job training.

*Where to study:* All major universities and Victorian College of Agriculture and Horticulture.

*Current workforce:* 46,000.

*Future prospects:* Moderate.

*Starting wage:* $600+.

*Wage after three years:* $820+.

*Further information:* NSW Association of Nurserymen Ltd, PO Box 13, Rouse Hill, NSW 2153.

Australian Institute of Horticulture, 257 Pacific Highway, Lindfield, NSW 2070.


## HOTELS AND CATERING

One of the major industries in Australia, particularly in tourist areas. Opportunities exist for bartenders, chambermaids/chambermen, kitchen hands and waiters and waitresses on both a casual and permanent basis. However, experience is often preferred, especially in these times of recession where employers are looking for stability rather than people who are going to be moving on after a few weeks.

On a vocational level there are openings for managers, personnel managers, front office managers, executive chefs, executive house-keepers and chief engineers. These careers can all be trained for in Australia.

*Qualifications:* Degree or Associate Diploma.

*Where to study:* Most major universities plus private colleges including Macleay College (which offers a highly regarded Hospitality Management course), Blue Mountains International Hotel MGNT School, Kenvale College, Australian College of Travel and Hospitality, Bill Healy Travel School, Macquarie Commercial College, Australian Business Academy, Cairns Business College, Gold Coast College of Business, Australian International College of Commerce.

*Current workforce* (hotel management): 30,000.

*Future prospects:* Good, particularly for well-trained and qualified professionals at all levels.

*Starting wage:* From $400+.

*Wage after three years:* From $450+.

*Further information:* Catering Institute of Australia, GPO Box 157, Sydney, NSW 2001.

National Tourism Industry Training Committee, 3rd Floor, 541 George Street, Sydney, NSW 2000.

## INDUSTRIAL DESIGN

Concerned with the design of products for manufacturing industry. Designers work for the manufactures or private consultancies.

*Qualifications:* Degree.

*Where to study:* Universities of Canberra, New South Wales, Newcastle, South Australia and Western Australia and Curtain University of Technology, La Trobe University of Northern Victoria, and Queensland University of Technology.

*Current workforce:* 1,400.

*Future prospects:* Good.

*Starting wage:* $550+.

*Wage after three years:* $710+.

*Further information:* Australian Design Council, 2-6 Cavill Avenue, Ashfield, 2137.

Design Institute of Australia, 220 Pacific Highway, Crows Nest.

## INSURANCE

A variety of occupations exist in the areas of life insurance, fire, marine and accident insurance, and health insurance. The latter has undergone tremendous expansion over the last few years and it is still a major growth industry.

*Qualifications:* Degree, Certificate and/or on-the-job training.

*Where to study:* Most major universities, TAFE colleges and the Australian Traineeship Scheme.

*Current workforce* (including brokers, agents, officers and clerks): 44,000.

*Future prospects:* Good.

*Starting wage:* $600+.

*Wage after three years:* $745+.

*Further information:* Insurance Institute of NSW, Level 1, 20 Bridge Street, Sydney, NSW 2000.

## INTERIOR DESIGN

These designers work with manufacturers, suppliers and contractors.

*Qualifications:* Degree or Diploma.
*Where to study:* Curtain University, Griffith University, Queensland College of Art, Queensland University of Technology, University of South Australia, University of Technology Sydney, Victoria University of Technology.
*Current workforce:* 1,000.
*Future prospects:* Good.
*Starting wage:* $560.
*Wage after three years:* $720+.
*Further information:* Design of Australia, GPO Box 9883, Sydney, NSW 2000.

## JEWELLERY AND GEMMOLOGY

More openings exist than in many countries since Australia is one of the biggest producers of gems in the world. A gemmologist studies stones to find out what type they are, whether they have been treated in any way, and to identify how best they can be cut. Specialised training is vital.

*Qualifications/training:* Degree, Diploma, Associate Diploma and apprenticeship certificate courses.
*Where to study:* Griffith University, Queensland College of Art, University of Tasmania, Victoria College of Technology, and TAFE colleges in all states.
*Current workforce:* 4,500.
*Future prospects:* Fair.
*Starting wage:* $460+.
*Wage after three years:* $540+.
*Further information:* Jewellers Association of Australia Ltd, Federal Secretariat, PO Box E 446 Queen Victoria Terrace, Canberra, ACT 2600.

## JOURNALISM

British journalists looking to find work in Australia would be well advised to get hold of a number of Australian publications first. The style of journalism is slightly different from the British variety; it tends to be more direct and colloquial.

Minimum rates of pay are fixed by an industrial award and journalists are promoted from a D grade up to the top level of A grade.

*Qualifications/training:* University degree or cadetship. There are two types of cadetship — people without a degree will need to undertake three or four years training while for a degree-holder this will probably be cut to one year.

*Where to study:* Unlike Britain there are a wide range of journalism courses throughout Australia. They are run by most major universities and also the privately run Macleay College.

*Current workforce:* 14,000.

*Future prospects:* Good.

*Starting wage:* $570+.

*Wage after three years:* $825+.

*Further information:* The Australian Journalists' Association, 403 Elizabeth Street, Sydney, NSW 2000.

## LAW

This is one profession which may require conversions for British qualifications. There are numerous places to do this but an initial approach to The Law Society of NSW, 170 Philip Street, Sydney, NSW 2000 would be a good idea. There are currently 27,000 people working in various aspects of the Australian legal profession and prospects look good.

## LIBRARIAN

*Qualifications:* Degree and Graduate Diploma, Associate Diploma.

*Where to study:* Ballarat University College, Charles Sturt University, Curtain University, Edith Cowan University, Monash University College, Northern Territory University, universities of Canberra, Melbourne and South Australia and TAFE colleges in all states.

*Current workforce:* 11,000.

*Future prospects:* Average.

*Starting wage:* $600+.

*Wage after three years:* $725+.
*Further information:* The Australian Library and Information Association, PO Box E441, Queen Victoria Terrace, ACT 2601.

## LOCKSMITH

*Training:* Apprenticeship.
*Where to study:* TAFE colleges in all states.
*Current workforce:* 1,400.
*Future prospects:* Good.
*Starting wage:* $550+.
*Wage after three years:* $625+.
*Further information:* Master Locksmith's Association in individual states.

## MEDICINE

With 23-30 areas of specialisation there are numerous avenues for medical staff. Although prospects for doctors are above average, staff turnover is low and produces relatively few vacancies.

*Qualifications:* Degree.
*Where to study:* Universities of Adelaide, Melbourne, New South Wales, Newcastle, Queensland, Sydney, Tasmania and Western Australia.
*Current workforce:* 47,000.
*Future prospects:* Good.
*Starting wage:* $880+.
*Wage after three years:* $1200+.
*Further information:* The Australian Medical Association, AMA House, 33 Atchison Street, St Leonards, NSW.

## METAL TRADES

These cover boilermakers, fitters, machinists, welders, toolmakers and sheet metal workers.
*Training:* All metal trades are entered by three to four year apprenticeships. These consist of practical training and part-time technical courses.
*Where to study:* TAFE colleges in all states.
*Future prospects:* Good for toolmakers, metal fitters and machinists but bleaker for other professions.

## MINING

Coal mining in Australia has been badly hit by the world recession and the fall in demand for coal. Competition for jobs is now fierce.

*Training:* On-the-job training.
*Current workforce:* 15,000.
*Future prospects:* Moderate – poor.
*Starting wage:* $500+.
*Wage after three years:* $680+.
*Further information:* Miners' Federation, 377 Sussex Street, Sydney, NSW 2000.
Joint Coal Board, 1 Chifley Square, Sydney, NSW 2000.

## MOTHERCRAFT NURSING

This involves the care of babies and pre-school children, liaising with parents and families. Two courses of training can be undertaken for mothercraft nursing, a short one of six months and a longer one of twelve months.

*Training:* Private college courses.
*Where to study:* The Karitane Mothercraft Society, Tresillian Training Homes.
*Current workforce:* 90,000.
*Future prospects:* Very good.
*Starting wage:* $390+.
*Wage after three years:* $500+.
*Further information:* The Karitane Mothercraft Society, Karitane Training Centre, PO Box 67, Randwick, 2031.
Tresillian Training Homes, 2 Shaw Street, Petersham 2049.

## MOTOR TRADE

Australians are heavily into motor vehicles and this has spawned a motor industry with an assortment of careers including: mechanics, panel beaters, vehicle painters, trimmers, brake mechanics and salesmen. However, although there are over 7000 outlets for new cars the employment situation is somewhat static presently, due mainly to a drop in the sales of new cars.

*Training:* Most jobs in the motor industry are entered through apprenticeships and on-the-job training.
*Where to study:* TAFE colleges in all states.

*Current workforce:* 147,000.
*Future prospects:* Average.
*Starting wage:* $260+.
*Wage after three years:* $480+.
*Further information:* Vehicle Builders Employees' Federation of Australia, Suite 1, 8th Floor, Labor Council Building, 377-383 Sussex Street, Sydney, NSW 2000.

Motor Traders' Association of NSW, 43 Brisbane Street, Sydney, NSW 2000. Motor Vehicle Repair Industry Council, 239 Great North Road, Five Dock, NSW.

## MUSIC

Similar to drama in that there are a reasonable number of musicians in Australia. Talent will always rise to the top. There are a number of categories to be considered: composers, performers, musicologists and music administrators. Most of these require some form of tertiary education.

*Qualifications:* Degree or Associate Diploma.
*Where to study:* Most universities in Australia have music courses.
*Current workforce:* 5,500.
*Future prospects:* Moderate.
*Starting wage:* $600+.
*Wage after three years:* $700+.
*Further information:* The Musicians' Union of Australia, 5th Floor, Labor Council Building, 377-383 Sussex Street, Sydney, NSW.

## NATURAL THERAPY

A form of medicine, based on the theory that prevention is better than cure. It is not a recognised health profession and individual professional associations set standards for membership.

*Training:* A full-time, four year course at private colleges.
*Where to study:* Consult the Australian Natural Therapists Association and the Australian Traditional Medicine Society for relevant courses.
*Current workforce:* 600.
*Future prospects:* Average.
*Starting wage:* $650+.
*Wage after three years:* $750+.

*Further information:* Australian Natural Therapists Association (ANTA), PO Box 522, Sutherland NSW 2232.
The Australian Traditional Medicine Society Limited, PO Box 442, Ryde, NSW 2112.

## NURSE (REGISTERED)

Undertake similar work to the nursing profession in Britain.

*Qualifications:* Diploma or Degree.
*Where to study:* Most universities in Australia.
*Current workforce:* 130,000.
*Future prospects:* Average.
*Starting wage:* $540+.
*Wage after three years:* $670+.
*Further information:* Nursing Careers Adviser, NSW Health Department, 73 Miller Street, North Sydney, NSW 2060.

## NURSE (ENROLLED)

They work directly under registered nurses. They also work in the community, carrying out various duties in the homes of patients.

*Training:* On-the-job training and TAFE courses.
*Where to study:* TAFE colleges in all states.
*Current workforce:* 43,000.
*Future prospects:* Average.
*Starting wage:* $385+.
*Wage after three years:* $510+.
*Further information:* Nursing Careers Adviser, NSW Health Department, 73 Miller Street, North Sydney, NSW 2060.

## OCCUPATIONAL THERAPY

This type of therapist works in hospitals, rehabilitation centres, special schools for children, psychiatric facilities, community health centres, nursing homes and private practices. New areas are currently being developed for occupational therapists; reform and penal institutions, preventative and rehabilitative work in industry, education in the best use of leisure time, education for creative retirement, and programmes for the unemployed.

*Qualifications:* Degree.
*Where to study:* Curtain University, La Trobe University and the universities of Newcastle, Queensland, South Australia and Sydney.
*Current workforce:* 4,000.
*Future prospects:* Very good.
*Starting wage:* $690+.
*Wage after three years:* $820+.
*Further information:* NSW Association of Occupational Therapists, PO Box 142, Ryde, NSW 2112.

## OIL DRILLER

The oil industry is in a similar volatile state as the mining business and it is hard to predict what will happen in the future. Most oil companies do take on unskilled platform workers and the best way to get these jobs is to be in the right area when they are recruiting.

*Training:* On-the-job and courses run by the Australian Drilling Industry Training Committee.
*Where to study:* On-the-job.
*Current workforce:* 15,000.
*Future prospects:* Average.
*Starting wage:* $685+.
*Wage after three years:* $800+.
*Further information:* Australian Drilling Industry Training Committee, Box 1545, Macquarie Centre, NSW 2113.

## OPTOMETRIST

*Qualifications:* Degree.
*Where to study:* Universities of Melbourne, New South Wales, Sydney and La Trobe.
*Current workforce:* 1,900.
*Future prospects:* Good.
*Starting wage:* $780+.
*Wage after three years:* $920+.
*Further information:* Australian Optometrical Association, Level 8, 26 Ridge Street, North Sydney, NSW 2060.

## ORTHOPTIST

This is a health profession which deals with visual and ocular motor anomalies. These include squints, cross-eyes and diseases of the eyes such as defective binocular vision (use of two eyes as a pair).

*Qualifications:* Degree.
*Where to study:* La Trobe University, University of Sydney — Cumberland College of Health Sciences.
*Current workforce:* 300.
*Future prospects:* Good.
*Starting wage:* $840+.
*Wage after three years:* $1060+
*Further information:* As above and The Orthoptic Clinic, Sydney Eye Hospital, Sir John Young Crescent, Woolloomooloo, NSW.

## OPTICAL DISPENSER

Deals with fitting spectacles from an optometrist's prescription.

*Qualifications:* TAFE Advanced Certificate or Guild of Dispensing Opticians diploma.
*Where to study:* TAFE colleges in all states.
*Current workforce:* 1,000.
*Future prospects:* Good.
*Further information:* Guild of Dispensing Opticians, 12 Thomas Street, Chatswood, NSW 2067.

## OPTICAL MECHANIC

The person responsible for grinding lenses and assembling spectacles.

*Training:* Apprenticeship.
*Where to study:* TAFE colleges in all states.
*Current workforce:* 1000+.
*Future prospects:* Average.
*Starting wage:* $300+.
*Wage after three years:* $550+.
*Further information:* Optical Prescriptions Spectacle Makers Pty Ltd, 66 Reservoir Street, Surry Hills, NSW 2010.

## ORGANISATION AND METHODS ANALYST

These analysts carry out studies intended to improve efficiency in businesses and government departments.

*Training:* Usually on-the-job. Most O and M analysts come from other disciplines such as personnel or accounts. A degree or associate diploma in business management, business administration, personnel or economics.

*Where to study:* Specific courses are available at Bond University, Deakin University, Griffith University, Queensland University of Technology, University of New South Wales, Victorian University of Technology — RMIT. Other courses in administration and business studies are available from most other Australian universities.

*Current workforce:* 3000.

*Future prospects:* Average.

*Starting wage:* $660+.

*Wage after three years:* $870+.

*Further information:* Any Careers Reference Centre or CES Work Information Centre.

## PATTERNMAKING

A patternmaker produces the pattern from which engineers create such products as cylinder blocks, baths, sinks and ships' propellors. Much of the art of the patternmaker has been taken over by computers.

*Training:* Apprenticeship.

*Where to study:* TAFE colleges in all states.

*Current workforce:* 1,000.

*Future prospects:* Poor.

*Starting wage:* $300+.

*Wage after three years:* $520+.

*Further information:* Master Patternmaking Section, Metal Trades Industry Association of Australia, NSW Branch, 51 Walker Street, North Sydney, NSW 2060.

## PERSONNEL OFFICER

Deals with all aspects of employing people: manpower planning, recruiting and selecting, wage and salary administration, training and development, pensions, welfare activities, pensions, medical checks and health and safety regulations. They also deal with problems that occur with employees at work. There are various categories within the range of personnel; managers, specialists, and clerks.

*Qualifications/training:* Degree, TAFE Certificate and on-the-job training.
*Where to study:* Most major universities in Australia and TAFE colleges in all states.
*Current workforce:* Managers: 5000. Specialists: 16,000. Clerks: 15,000.
*Future prospects:* Good.
*Starting wage* (Clerks): $440+.
*Wage after three years:* $620+.
*Further information:* Institute of Personnel Management, 4 Waters Road, Neutral Bay, NSW 1089.

## PHARMACIST

Similar to the work of pharmacists in Britain, employed in community practice, hospitals or the pharmaceutical industry.

*Qualifications:* Degree.
*Where to study:* Curtain University of Technology, Victorian College of Pharmacy, and universities of Queensland, South Australia, Sydney and Tasmania.
*Current workforce:* 11,000.
*Future prospects:* Average.
*Starting wage:* $720+.
*Wage after three years:* $900+.
*Further information:* Pharmaceutical Society of Australia, 82 Christie Street, St. Leonards, NSW.

## PHOTOGRAPHER

There is a wide range of photographic possibilities including commercial, advertising, fashion, portraiture, newspaper, industrial, and scientific.

*Qualifications/training:* Degree, Diploma, Associate Diploma, TAFE Certificates and private college courses.
*Where to study:* Charles Sturt University, Griffith University, James Cook

University of North Queensland, Northern Territory University, Queensland College of Art, University of New South Wales, College of Fine Arts, University of South Australia, University of Western Australia, Victoria College, Australian Centre of Photography, Photography Studies College (Melbourne), Australian College of Photography, Arts and Communications and TAFE colleges in all states.

*Current workforce:* 8,300.

*Future prospects:* Good.

*Starting wage:* $575+.

*Wage after three years:* $700+.

*Further information:* Australian Institute of Professional Photographers, 49 Samuel Street, Ryde, NSW.

## PHYSICAL FITNESS INSTRUCTOR

Since Australia is such a health conscious nation there are a wide range of health clubs and centres in all states.

*Qualifications:* Degree, Associate Diploma or TAFE Certificate.

*Where to study:* Australian College of Physical Education, and most major universities.

*Current workforce:* 20,000.

*Future prospects:* Very good.

*Starting wage:* $300+.

*Wage after three years:* $550+.

*Further information:* Australian Council for Health, Physical Education and Recreation, PO Box 84, Croydon, NSW 2132.

## PHYSIOTHERAPIST

Australia has some of the best physiotherapy training in the world.

*Qualifications:* Degree.

*Where to study:* Curtain University, La Trobe University, universities of Melbourne, Newcastle, Queensland, South Australia and Sydney (Cumberland College of Health Sciences).

*Current workforce:* 7,500.

*Future prospects:* Very good.

*Starting wage:* $720+.

*Wage after three years:* $850+.

*Further information:* Australian Physiotherapy Association, 112 Majors Bay Road, Concord, NSW.

## PODIATRIST

Formerly called chiropodists, podiatrists deal with ailments and diseases of the feet. Many set up their own practices but to do this they must first register with the state.

*Qualifications:* Degree or Diploma.
*Where to study:* Curtain University, La Trobe University, Queensland University of Technology and University of South Australia.
*Current workforce:* 1,200.
*Future prospects:* Very good.
*Starting wage:* $600+
*Wage after three years:* $750+.
*Further information:* Australian Podiatry Association, 446 Elizabeth Street, Sydney, NSW 2000.

## POLICE FORCE

### Australian Federal Police Force (AFP)

In addition to domestic duties the Australian Federal Police Force provides men for the UN Peace Keeping Force in Cyprus. Applicants must be between the ages of 18 and 35 and be in good physical health. They should also be Australian citizens.

*Qualifications/training:* Graduates with degrees in economics, accountancy, computing, law and science are in great demand. The minimum requirement is completion of Year 12 at school. Training is undertaken at the Police Headquarters in Canberra. This consists of a sixteen week orientation, theory and practical course and then officers are posted to either Sydney, Melbourne or Canberra for further on-the-job training.
*Current workforce:* 200 new recruits are taken every year.
*Future prospects:* Good.
*Starting wage:* $430+.
*Wage after three years:* $620+.
*Further information:* Australian Federal Police Recruitment Consultant, GPO Box 2845, Canberra City, ACT 2601.

### New South Wales Police

State police forces have similar requirements to the Federal ones. In NSW training consists of an eighteen month Police Recruitment

Education Programme, involving study and on-the-job training. This is undertaken at the NSW Police Academy at Goulburn.

*Current workforce:* 35,000.
*Future prospects:* Good.
*Starting wage:* $430+.
*Wage after three years:* $620+.
*Further information:* Recruiting Officer, Police Headquarters, 14-24 College Street, Sydney, NSW 2000.


## PRINTING

There are five main areas to consider: graphic reproduction operator, printing machinist, book binding, screen printing and table hand. The industry is still relatively labour intensive but in the next few years this could change due to advanced technology.

*Training:* Apprenticeship.
*Where to study:* TAFE colleges in all states.
*Current workforce* (total): 45,000.
*Future prospects:* Moderate.
*Starting wage:* $280+.
*Wage after three years:* $525+.
*Further information:* Printing and Allied Trades Employers' Federation of Australia, 77 Lithgow Street, St Leonards, NSW.


## PRISON OFFICER

A minimum age of 20 years is required and all training is done within the service.

*Training:* Twelve week full-time course.
*Where to study:* Prison Service.
*Current workforce:* 8,000.
*Future prospects:* Good.
*Starting wage:* $630+.
*Wage after three years:* $710+.
*Further information:* Probation and Parole Service, Department of Corrective Services, Roden Cutler House, 24 Campbell Street, Sydney, NSW 2000.
Recruitment Division, NSW Public Service, Goodsell Building, 8-12 Chifley Square, Sydney NSW, 2000.

## PSYCHOLOGIST

A wide range of openings exist for trained psychologists: clinical, counselling, vocational, community, organisational, educational, research and applied sports. Due to cutbacks in some social welfare expenditure competition for jobs is getting fiercer, although extensive growth is expected in this field.

*Qualifications:* Degree — a four years honours degree is needed for admission to the Australian Psychological Society.
*Where to study:* Most major universities in Australia.
*Current workforce:* 4,900.
*Future prospects:* Very good.
*Starting wage:* $730+.
*Wage after three years:* $880+.
*Further information:* Australian Psychological Society, 30 Atchison Street, St Leonards, NSW.

## PUBLIC RELATIONS

PR work is available across the whole spectrum of government and private companies. There are a number of degree and certificate courses on offer, but not all are recognised by the Public Relations Institute of Australia (PRIA) which represents about 25 per cent of practitioners. Before you start a course it is wise to check with your state office of PRIA. Graduates are preferred for employment in consultancies.

*Qualifications:* Degree or TAFE Certificate for sub-professional entry.
*Where to study:* Bond University, Charles Sturt University, Deakin University, Edith Cowan University, Queensland University of Technology, Victoria University of Technology, University College of Central Queensland, University of Canberra, University of New England, University of Western Australia, TAFE colleges in all states and the private Macleay College.
*Current workforce:* 22,500.
*Future prospects:* Very good.
*Starting wage:* $650+.
*Wage after three years:* $800+.
*Further information:* Public Relations Institute of Australia, PO Box 1728, North Sydney, NSW 2025.

## PUBLIC SERVICE

As with the British Civil Service the Australian Public Service (APS) cover a wide range of occupations and professions. Most of them are office based. Some of the areas covered are economic management, foreign affairs, trade, productivity and industry, community services, social security, health, education, territorial administration, transport, employment and industrial relations, environmental concerns, Aboriginal affairs, arts, heritage, and agricultural and fisheries policies.

There are over 180,000 public servants and they fill all kinds of jobs: administrative service officers, computer systems officers, office machine operators (typists, stenographers and wordprocessor operators), data processing operators and technical officers. There are openings for graduates and non-graduates alike. Selection is based on academic qualifications, a selection test and an interview. There are also a number of openings for handicapped applicants.

A number of universities offer degree courses in public administration: Charles Sturt University, Curtain University, Griffith University, Murdoch University, Northern Territory University, Philip Institute of Technology, Queensland University of Technology, University College of Central Queensland and universities of Canberra, New England and Queensland.

*Further information:* Public Sector Recruitment Office, 17th Floor, Two Hall House, 456 Kent Street, Sydney, NSW 2000.


## QUANTITY SURVEYOR

These professionals can either work for themselves as consultants, or for building contractors, developers or government departments or agencies. Qualifications gained in Australia are recognised worldwide.

*Qualifications:* Degree.
*Where to study:* Most major universities.
*Current workforce:* 1,400.
*Future prospects:* Average.
*Starting wage:* $630+.
*Wage after three years:* $825+.
*Further information:* Australian Institute of Quantity Surveyors, National Surveyors House, 27-29 Napier Close, Deakin, ACT 2600.

## RADIOGRAPHERS

This job falls into two main categories, diagnostic and therapeutic. Employment is mainly in hospitals and private practices, and also public health services and industry for diagnostic radiographers. There are a number of courses available and these are governed by the Royal Australian College of Radiologists and the Australian Institute of Radiography.

*Qualifications:* Degree, Diploma.
*Where to study:* Charles Sturt University, Curtain University, Queensland University of Technology, and universities of Newcastle, South Sydney, Sydney (Cumberland College of Health Sciences) and Tasmania.
*Current workforce:* 4,000.
*Future prospects:* Very good.
*Starting wage:* $680+.
*Wage after three years:* $900+.
*Further information:* Australian Institute of Radiography, PO Box 2426, North Paramatta, NSW 2151.

## RADIO/TV REPAIRER

With advanced technology this also covers the repair of hi-fis, business machines, word processors and videos.

*Training:* Apprenticeship.
*Where to study:* TAFE colleges in all states.
*Current workforce:* 6,000.
*Future prospects:* Average.
*Starting wage:* $320+.
*Wage after three years:* $560+.
*Further information:* Electrical Contractors' Association, 51 William Street, Sydney, NSW 2000; 155 Wellington Parade South, Jolimont 3002, Victoria; 213 Greenhill Road, Eastwood 5063, South Australia; 51 Berwick Street, Fortitude Valley 4006, Queensland; PO Box 364, Canberra 2601, ACT; GPO Box 1544R, West Perth 6005, Western Australia.

## RANGER

Work in all areas of conservation and management in National Parks and the Wildlife Service.

*Qualifications:* Degree or Associate Diploma.
*Where to study:* Most major universities.
*Current workforce:* 1,000.
*Future prospects:* Average.
*Further information:* National Parks and Wildlife Service, 43 Bridge Street, Hurtsville, NSW.
Ministry for Conservation, 240 Victoria Parade, East Melbourne, Victoria.

## RECEPTIONIST

Good employment prospects in all major cities for receptionists with good training and experience.

*Qualifications:* Certificate and private college courses.
*Where to study:* Metropolitan Business College and TAFE colleges in all states.
*Current workforce:* 137,500.
*Future prospects:* Average.
*Starting wage:* $300.
*Wage after three years:* $460+.
*Further information:* TAFE Information Centres in all states.

## RECREATION OFFICERS

As increasing emphasis is being put on the use of leisure time this is one area which could show significant growth in the future. Recreation officers are employed by the Department of Sport and Recreation in various states, by city councils, organisations such as the YMCA and YWCA and psychiatric hospitals.

*Qualifications:* Degree or Diploma.
*Where to study:* Universities of Canberra, New South Wales, Newcastle, Queensland, South Australia and Wollongong, Charles Sturt University, Edith Cowan University, Griffith University, James Cook University of North Queensland, La Trobe University and the Australian College of Physical Education.
*Current workforce:* 3,000.
*Future prospects:* Good.
*Starting wage:* $600.
*Wage after three years:* $740+.

*Further information:* NSW Department of Sport, Recreation and Racing, Head Office, 105 Miller Street, North Sydney, NSW 2060.

## REAL ESTATE

This includes property managers and real estate salespersons.

*Qualifications:* Certificate of Registration, Advanced Certificate and Degree courses.
*Where to study:* Real Estate Institutes in all states, TAFE colleges in all states and Bond University, Curtain University, Queensland University of Technology, and University of Queensland, University of South Australia, University of Technology, Sydney, Victorian University of Technology — RMIT.
*Current workforce:* 45,000.
*Future prospects:* Average.
*Starting wage:* $400+.
*Wage after three years:* $580+.
*Further information:* Real Estate Institute of NSW, 30-32 Wentworth Avenue, Sydney, NSW 2000.

## REFRIGERATION/AIR CONDITIONING MECHANICS

Australians like everything to be cool, whether it is their beer or their homes. This means that there is always plenty of work for this group of mechanics.

*Training:* Apprenticeship and TAFE courses.
*Where to study:* On-the-job training and TAFE colleges in all states.
*Current workforce:* 10,500.
*Future prospects:* Good.
*Starting wage after training:* $525+.
*Further information:* The Metal Industry Association of Australia, 51 Walker Street, North Sydney, NSW.
The Australian Institute of Refrigeration, Air-conditioning and Heating, 104 Paramatta Road, Homebush, NSW.
The Refrigeration and Air-conditioning Contractors Association, Box 118, Post Office, Flemington Markets, NSW 2129.

## RETAILING

### Retail buyer
Responsible for buying goods from wholesalers and then passing them on for sale to the public.

*Training:* On-the-job in the form of a trainee managership.
*Current workforce:* 3,000.
*Future prospects:* Average.
*Starting wage:* $410+.
*Wage after three years:* $580+.
*Further information:* Retail Traders Association of NSW, 20 York Street, Sydney, NSW 2000. Also personnel departments of large retailers.

### Sales assistants
*Training:* On-the-job.
*Current workforce:* 233,000.
*Future prospects:* Good.
*Starting wage:* $300+.
*Wage after three years:* $440+.
*Further information:* As above.

## SECRETARIAL

The secretarial world has developed to a point where it embraces stenographers, word processor operators and data preparation operators. Top secretaries can progress to become private secretaries or executive assistants.

### Secretaries/Stenographers
*Qualifications:* Degree, Associate Diploma, TAFE Certificate and TAFE courses.
*Where to study:* TAFE courses in all states, Curtain University, University of New England, University of South Australia and the National Business College — NBC offers a 42 week Diploma course in Secretarial Studies.
*Current workforce:* 195,000.
*Future prospects:* Good.
*Starting wage:* $370+.
*Wage after three years:* $620+.
*Further information:* TAFE colleges in all states.

### Word Processor Operators/Data Preparation Operators
*Training:* TAFE and private college courses.
*Where to study:* As above.
*Current workforce:* 110,000+.
*Future prospects:* Very Good.
*Starting wage:* $350+.
*Wage after three years:* $525+.
*Further information:* As above.


## SOCIAL WORKER

Most Australian social workers are employed by the government, hospitals and private agencies such as the Royal Blind Society.

*Qualifications:* Degree — a four year course is offered in all states.
*Where to study:* Australian Catholic University, Avondale College, Bachelor College, Charles Sturt University, Curtain University, Flinders University of South Australia, James Cook University, Phillip Institute of Technology, Monash University, Queensland University of Technology, La Trobe, and universities of Sydney, New South Wales, Queensland, South Australia, Melbourne and Western Australia.
*Current workforce:* 11,400.
*Future prospects:* Average.
*Starting wage:* $650+.
*Wage after three years:* $780+.
*Further information:* Association of Social Workers, 66 Albion Street, Surry Hills, NSW 2010.


## SPEECH PATHOLOGIST

Deals with all areas of speech disorders.

*Qualifications:* Degree.
*Where to study:* Curtain University, University of Sydney — Cumberland College of Health Sciences.
*Current workforce:* 1,900.
*Future prospects:* Very good.
*Starting wage:* $750+
*Wage after three years:* $870+.
*Further information:* The Australian Association of Speech and Hearing, 112 Majors Bay Road, Concord, NSW.

## STOCK AND STATION AGENT

This is a job which involves sales of goods connected with farming: live-stock, machinery and fertiliser. The industry is dominated by a few large companies and most employees come from the country areas and have farming experience.

*Training:* TAFE courses and on-the-job training.
*Where to study:* TAFE courses in all states and rural studies courses at Charles Sturt University, La Trobe University, University of New England — Orange Agricultural College, University of New South Wales, University of Queensland — Gatton College and Victorian College of Agriculture and Horticulture.
*Starting wage:* $390+.
*Wage after three years:* $580+.
*Further information:* The Stock and Station Agents Association of NSW, Homebush Saleyards, Homebush, NSW.

## STOCK EXCHANGE

The careers encompassed by the Australian Stock Exchange include: juniors (reception and typing), intermediate (departmental secretaries), secretarial and stenographers, clerical, script clerks, accounts staff and research staff. There are also stock exchange operators, who usually work for stock brokers and represent their firms on the floor of the Stock Exchange. This involves using the **Stock Exchange Automated Trading System** (SEATS).

*Qualifications:* Degree, graduate Diploma, Certificate, and on-the-job training.
*Where to study:* Securities Institute of Australia.
*Current workforce:* 22,000.
*Future prospects:* Good.
*Starting wage:* $450+.
*Wage after three years:* $740+.
*Further information:* Securities Institute of Australia, Exchange Centre, 20 Bond Street, Sydney, NSW 2000.

## TEACHER

There are a wide range of possibilities for teachers, covering the usual areas of pre-primary teaching, primary teaching, secondary teaching, further education teaching and the teaching of exceptional children, including physically and mentally handicapped. Demand for teachers varies from state to state and good qualifications and/or experience are required.

*Qualifications:* Degree and a Teaching Diploma.
*Where to study:* Most universities in Australia.
*Current workforce:* Pre-primary 14,000. Primary 128,000. Secondary 107,000. Special education 4,500.
*Future prospects:* Average.
*Starting wage:* $575+.
*Wage after three years:* $750+.
*Further information:* Teachers Federation branches in individual states.

## TEXTILE DESIGNER

*Qualifications:* Degree, Associate Diploma.
*Where to study:* Charles Sturt University, University of New South Wales, University of Newcastle, TAFE colleges in NSW, VIC and ACT.
*Current workforce:* Very small.
*Future prospects:* Good.
*Starting wage:* $530+.
*Wage after three years:* $670+.

## TOWN PLANNER

They are employed by all levels of government.

*Qualifications:* Degree.
*Where to study:* Curtain University, Queensland University of Technology, Victoria University of Technology and universities of Melbourne, New England, New South Wales, Queensland, South Australia and Tasmania.
*Current workforce:* 3,000.
*Future prospects:* Good.
*Starting wage:* $600+.
*Wage after three years:* $800+.
*Further information:* The Australian Planning Institute, Darlinghurst Public School Annexe, Cnr. Barcom Avenue and Liverpool Street, Darlinghurst, NSW 2011.

## TRAIN DRIVER

The number of new recruits and trainees being taken on by Australian rail authorities is low, as is turnover of staff in existing jobs.

*Training:* Traineeship.
*Where to study:* On-the-job training.
*Current workforce:* 10,800.
*Future prospects:* Moderate.
*Starting wage:* $450+.
*Wage after three years:* $560+.
*Further information:* State Railway Authorities in all states.

## TRAVEL CONSULTANT

Another expanding profession thanks to the expansion of the leisure business.

*Qualifications:* Degree, Associate Diploma, Certificate and private college courses.
*Where to study:* Ballarat University College, Bond University, Charles Sturt University, Edith Cowan University, Griffith University, James Cook University of Northern Queensland, Monash University, Footscray Institute of Technology and universities of Canberra, New England, Queensland and Sydney. Also private courses at Metropolitan Business College.
*Current workforce:* 16,200.
*Future prospects:* Good.
*Starting wage:* $310+.
*Wage after three years:* $480+.
*Further information:* National Tourism Industry Training Committee, 3rd Floor, 541 George Street, Sydney, NSW 2000.

## VALUER

Deals with assessing the value of land and buildings, based on the current economic climate.

*Qualifications:* Valuers Certificate of Registration, Associate Diploma and Degree courses in Land Economy.
*Where to study:* Real Estate Institutes, TAFE colleges in all states, Bond University, Curtain University, and universities of Queensland, South Australia and Sydney.

*Current workforce:* 3,000.
*Future prospects:* Average.
*Starting wage:* $370+.
*Wage after three years:* $620+.
*Further information:* Australian Institute of Valuers and Land Economists, 300 George Street, Sydney, NSW 2000.

## VISUAL MERCHANDISING

Including both visual merchandisers and ticket writers this profession is concerned with presenting goods in an attractive fashion to the buying public. This covers window dressing and posters for point of sale advertising.

*Qualifications:* Certificate courses and on-the-job training.
*Where to train:* TAFE colleges in all states.
*Current workforce:* 2,500.
*Future prospects:* Good.
*Starting wage:* $390+.
*Wage after three years:* $550+.
*Further information:* Retail Training Council, PO Box C154, Clarence Street, Sydney, NSW 2000.

## WINE MAKER

Australia produces some of the best wines in the world and the wineries of Victoria, New South Wales, South Australia and Western Australia are good starting points for prospective or qualified wine makers.

*Qualifications:* Degree or Associate Diploma.
*Where to study:* Charles Sturt University, University of Adelaide — Roseworthy Campus.
*Current workforce:* 200.
*Future prospects:* Good.
*Further information:* The above universities.

## WOOL CLASSER

This involves all aspects of wool preparation and classification in the shearing shed. All states have wool classing courses run by TAFE and also some Agricultural Pastoral Colleges. They vary in length from six months full-time to two years part-time.

*Qualifications:* Certificate and Associate Diploma courses.

*Where to study:* University of New England — Orange Agricultural College, University of New South Wales, Victorian College of Agriculture and Horticulture and TAFE colleges in all states.

*Current workforce:* 1,200.

*Future prospects:* Poor.

*Further information:* Australian Wool Corporation, 55 Clarence Street, Sydney, NSW 2000.

## ZOOLOGY — ANIMAL CARER

*Qualifications:* Certificate courses.

*Where to study:* TAFE colleges in all states.

*Current workforce:* 3,000.

*Future:* Average.

*Starting wage:* $280+.

*Wage after three years:* $375+.

*Further information:* TAFE Information Centres.

# 9

## Recognition of Overseas Skills and Qualifications

### NATIONAL OFFICE OF OVERSEAS SKILLS RECOGNITION (NOOSR)

In many professions there are no restrictions for foreign workers entering the Australian workplace. However, certain professions require their workers to be registered and possess the necessary qualifications. For people trained in Australia this is no problem but for workers trained in Britain this could pose difficulties. In order to address this question the Australian Government established the **National Office of Overseas Skills Recognition** (NOOSR) in 1989, in order to make it easier for overseas-qualified people to ease themselves into the Australian workplace.

The belief on which NOOSR was formed is to promote recognition of skills on the basis of demonstrated competence. The long term goal is to replace reliance solely on paper qualifications by assessment processes for skills and work experience. The recognition of these skills is done by:

- Simplifying administrative processes and improving flexibility between occupations in professional, para-professional, technical and trades areas.

- Giving a reasonable chance to all skilled workers by encouraging the development of consistent national skills standards which do not discriminate between skills gained in Australia or overseas.

- Improving the information, counselling and referral services necessary to give migrants and prospective migrants the support they deserve in order to make a choice of career.

- Developing fair, open and easily understandable skills assessment procedures.

- Providing improved support services, such as better access to education and training for bridging and refresher purposes, where these will assist migrants obtain recognition of their skills.

- Promoting occupational deregulation wherever possible.

## NOOSR's Client Service

NOOSR offers comparative and competency assessment services to professionally and technically qualified prospective migrants and to overseas-trained people already resident in Australia, in the following areas: architecture, computing, general academic qualifications, nursing, radiography, social welfare, technical occupations, dentistry, dietetics, occupational therapy, pharmacy, physiotherapy, podiatry, veterinary science and occupational English.

The service consists of giving clients advice, counselling, comparative assessment and referral services, all geared towards overcoming skill recognition difficulties in all professional, para-professional and technical occupations. They will also direct clients who need further qualifications to obtain full recognition skills.

NOOSR deals with 15,000 cases each year, the majority of them migrants who want to gain the relevant qualifications or have their current qualifications assessed. If migrants want to have their qualifications assessed they should write directly to NOOSR, asking for an application form. This should be completed and returned. The assessment can take anything from a few days to several months, depending on the types of qualification being dealt with. Approximately 73 per cent of all assessments are successful and a charge of no less than $A100 is levied for each assessment. The individual charges may change without notice.

*Contact address*
National Office of Overseas Skills Recognition
First Floor, Derwent House, University Avenue, Canberra City, ACT.
Postal Address: GPO Box 1407, Canberra City, ACT, 2601.
Tel: 06 276 8111. Fax: 06 276 7636 or visit the Web site at:
www.detya.gov.au/noosr/

## ASSESSMENT OF INDIVIDUAL PROFESSIONS AND CONVERSION OF QUALIFICATIONS

### Accountancy

Accountants working in Australia need to be members of either the **Australian Society of Certified Practising Accountants** (ASCPA) or the **Institute of Chartered Accountants in Australia** (ICAA). If you are an accountant wanting to migrate to Australia you must meet the ASCPA or the ICAA membership requirements in order to get the highest possible points score for skills on your points test. In order to do this you must hold an academic qualification comparable to an Australian Bachelor degree. Your degree must also meet the specific requirements of these two organisations.

However, it is virtually impossible for overseas-trained accountants to meet these membership needs immediately because both the ASCPA and the ICAA require a prospective member to be trained in Australian company law and Australian taxation law. Because of these requirements the Department of Immigration, Local Government and Ethnic Affairs will accept overseas-trained accountants for migration on the basis of their skills if their qualifications need only minor upgrading — three or fewer subjects to be studied at tertiary level to meet ASCPA or ICAA requirements.

You can have your current situation assessed by either organisation by writing to:

- Educational Assessment Officer, The Australian Society of CPAs, 170 Queen Street, Melbourne, Victoria 3000.

- National Education Co-ordinator, The Institute of Chartered Accountants in Australia, GPO Box 3921, Sydney, NSW 2001.

A fee of $A100 will be charged and you will need to provide: family name, full address, date and country of birth, name and address of present employer, brief employment history, the institution where you studied, course name and the award your received, duration of course, name of any professional accountancy organisations of which you are a member, certified copies of your original degree or certificate, a list of all subjects studied and grades awarded.

After the assessment the ASCPA or the ICAA will write to you and tell you whether your qualifications have been recognised and what upgrading you will require.

## Architecture

If you have overseas architectural qualifications these are assessed in Australia by the Architects Accreditation Council of Australia (AACA) in co-operation with NOOSR. General qualifications are evaluated under one of the following categories:

● Overseas qualifications considered equivalent to an approved architectural qualification in Australia, which are listed on the AACA Approved Overseas Architectural Qualifications List.

● Overseas qualifications not on the AACA Approved List but which have been accepted in individual cases in the past and are listed on the AACA Individually Approved Qualifications List.

These lists are held at AACA, who can be contacted by writing to:

● The Registrar, Architects Accreditation Council of Australia, PO Box 373, Manuka, ACT 2603.

If you apply from overseas your application should be sent to NOOSR, along with a $A100 fee. If you do not have your qualifications assessed as part of your migration then you should contact the Registrar of AACA when you arrive in Australia. If your qualifications are on the Approved List then you will be asked to contact a state or territory Registration Board to enquire about the requirements for registration. You will need to gain practical experience in Australia and also pass the AACA Architectural Practice Examination before you can register.

## Computing

Although there are no registration requirements for computer professionals in Australia and no formal minimum requirements it is a good idea to have qualifications which meet the minimum membership of the **Australian Computing Society** (ACS). This is currently an Associate Diploma, or alternatively you could sit the Society's Examination in Computing.

If you have trained as a computer professional overseas you will be assessed by NOOSR or according to NOOSR guidelines. If you apply before you enter Australia, as is recommended, you should send the following documentation: final certificate for academic awards, course transcript showing subjects studied and examination results, official employer references, dates of employment, details of major projects undertaken, the technology you have been using, your personal role in projects and software and computer equipment utilised.

You should include a fee of $A100 with you application and if you receive a favourable assessment from NOOSR then they will inform the Australian diplomatic mission where you have applied that you have met the minimum requirements to practise as a computer professional in Australia.

For further information contact NOOSR or the ACS at: PO Box 319, Darlinghurst, NSW 2010.

## Dentistry

The national professional body for dentists in Australia is the **Australian Dental Association** (ADA). Any registered dentist is eligible for membership.

If you have trained as a dentist overseas your qualifications may meet Australian requirements — qualifications from some British universities are immediately acceptable while others are not. If you are not eligible to be registered immediately then you can either take an Australian dental degree or sit written and clinical examinations conducted by the Australian Dental Examining Council (ADEC). You can take these examinations if you have completed four years' full-time academic training and you are in the process of migrating.

The ADEC examination consists of an English test, a preliminary examination and a clinical examination. The fee at the time of writing is $A2000 for all parts of the examination. If you pass you will then be eligible to apply for registration with any of the eight Australian dental boards.

Due to the cost involved in the ADEC examination it is a good idea to contact NOOSR first to see if it is necessary to sit it or not.

## Dietetics

Dietitians are only required to be registered to practise in Victoria and the Northern Territory; in the rest of Australia there are no legal limits on the practice of the profession. However, if you want to work in government-controlled hospitals you will be expected to have qualifications acceptable to the **Dietitians Association of Australia** (DAA), or the dietitians' boards of Victoria or Northern Territory. If you hold overseas qualifications then you will have to pass a NOOSR examination before being eligible for membership of the DAA or registration with the boards. You can only take this examination if you are a permanent resident of Australia, or if you are going through the migration procedures, or if you have been given permission to engage in employment in Australia.

In order to sit the Examination you should write to the Registrar of

Dietetic Qualifications at NOOSR and include: a certified copy of your degree, diploma or professional qualification, details of the course content, official evidence of any internships, official evidence of any registration/licensure, official evidence of extra qualifications and official evidence of any change of name. At the time of writing the fee for the Dietetics Examination is $A200.

### Nursing

The main national professional nursing body in Australia is the **Australian Nursing Federation** (ANF). To work as a nurse in Australia you must be registered with the nurse-registering authority in the state or territory where you intend to practise. If you have qualified as a nurse in a country with a health care delivery system similar to Australia's in culture, technology, licensing and language then you could be considered for immediate registration in Australia. The countries which meet these requirements are Canada, Ireland, New Zealand, South Africa, United Kingdom and the USA.

If you have been trained in the United Kingdom you can be registered after your arrival in Australia, in some cases, after only an interview with the registering authority. Registration fees range between $A25-40. You will need certified copies of all original nursing documents when you register.

For further information contact: Australian Nursing Federation, 373-375 St George's Road, North Fitzroy, Victoria 3068. Tel: 03 482 2722.

### Pharmacy

The **Australian Pharmacy Examining Council**, which is associated with NOOSR, was established to help pharmacists educated overseas to become registered in Australia so that they could practise their profession. The Council has established an examination for overseas-trained pharmacists to demonstrate that they have the knowledge to practise in Australia.

The Council examination is open to any pharmacist who has completed a pharmacy course which included at least three years' full-time academic study and is eligible for registration as a pharmacist in the country in which that qualification was obtained. You must also be eligible to migrate to Australia.

The council's examination procedure is as follows:

- Stage 1 examination — a written multiple-choice question examination covering basic pharmaceutical sciences. There are two papers, each taking two hours and consisting of 100 questions.

- Interview and counselling.

- Twelve months' supervised practice in an Australian pharmacy.

- Stage 2 examination — a practical and oral examination covering the practice of pharmacy.

The fee for the Stage 1 examination is $A250 and for the Stage 2 examination $A500. The average success rate is 60 per cent.

For further information contact NOOSR or: Executive Director, **Pharmaceutical Society of Australia,** 44 Thesiger Court, Deakin, ACT 2605.

## Physiotherapy

All practising physiotherapists in Australia must be registered with the relevant state or territory body. If not they cannot practise or use the title physiotherapist. Each state and territory has different registration laws and registration in one state does not automatically allow you to practise in another. To do this separate registration is required. The professional body is the **Australian Physiotherapy Association** (APA).

The Australian Examining Council for Overseas Physiotherapists Incorporated (AECOP) has a procedure whereby physiotherapists who qualified overseas may prove their competence to practise in Australia. If you are an overseas-educated physiotherapist you can apply to register in Australia if you obtain the AECOP Final Certificate.

To have your overseas qualifications assessed, you must complete an Application for Assessment form; these are available from Australian diplomatic posts, or AECOP and APA offices in Australia. You must apply as part of an application to migrate and once this application is accepted you can approach NOOSR with your application for assessment. You must also provide supporting documentation consisting of: your final diploma or degree, a transcript of your course, showing subjects and hours, examination results detailing practical, theoretical and clinical education, documented evidence of any internships, references or evidence of employment since your graduation, evidence of any registration/licensure, documented evidence of any change of name.

To be eligible to take the AECOP examination procedure you must satisfy them that:

- The physiotherapy course you took was similar in theory and practice to the physiotherapy curricula in Australia.

- The physiotherapy course included an appropriate electrotherapy component.

- Your course would qualify you to practise as a physiotherapist in the country where the course was taken.

- You completed at least two years' full-time postgraduate clinical practice or the equivalent part-time, within three years of the date of application. (If you qualified less than two years before your application then this does not apply.)

All eligible overseas physiotherapists applying for registration in Australia have to follow at least one of the following procedures:

1. Take the AECOP screening examination — two papers, each with approximately 150 multiple-choice questions. You can sit the examination at an overseas Australian Government office. The fee at the time of writing is $A200.

2. Supervised Clinical Practice.

3. The AECOP Clinical Examination. This is only available in Australia and it is recommended that supervised clinical practice is undertaken before this examination is sat. The fee at the time of writing is $A450.

For further information contact: The Executive Officer, Australian Examining Council for Overseas Physiotherapists, GPO Box 1407, Canberra City, ACT 2601.

### Podiatry

Each Australian state has separate legislation covering the recognition of podiatry qualifications. Registration in one state does not automatically make you eligible for registration in another. Each state has a registration board and NOOSR helps these boards to assess overseas-qualified podiatrists through an examination procedure. If you are an overseas-trained podiatrist you must take this examination. It consists of an English test, if needed, a Stage 1 examination — written, and a Stage 2 examination — clinical and oral.

There are three levels of eligibility for this NOOSR examination for podiatrists:

1.  If you have finished a three-year, full-time tertiary course from an institution in the United Kingdom, *and* you have current registration or you are eligible for registration in the country where you qualified, then you will only have to sit the Stage 2 examination.

2.  If you have completed at least a three-year, full-time tertiary course at an institution outside the United Kingdom *and* have current registration, then you will have to sit the Stage 1 and Stage 2 examinations.

3.  If you have had different but comparable podiatry training, this will be considered separately.

If you wish to take the podiatry examination you should apply for a form from NOOSR or your nearest Australian embassy or consulate. You must send certified copies of the following documents with your application: final diploma or degree obtained on completion of podiatry course, transcript of the course showing subjects and hours and detailing practical and theoretical examination results, evidence of further education and training, post graduate qualifications, evidence of registration/licensure, evidence of current registration, evidence of employment experience after graduation, two recent employment references, documented evidence of change of name where applicable.

The fee for the Stage 1 examination is $A200 while the fee for Stage 2 is $A450.

For further information write to NOOSR or contact: Executive Director, Australian Podiatry Council, Suite 11, 96 Camberwell Road, Hawthorn, Victoria 3122.

## Radiography

The organisation which represents the professional and ethical practice of radiography is **The Australian Institute of Radiography** (AIR), 212 Clarendon Street, East Melbourne, Victoria 3002.

To become a registered radiographer in Australia, you first have to meet the minimum entry requirements of all appropriate Australian tertiary institutions. Since 1986 this is a diploma-level course with at least three years' full-time study.

If you have an overseas qualification your application will be assessed through NOOSR and you will be advised in one of the following ways:

●   You could be advised that your qualifications, training and experience in radiography make you eligible for membership of the AIR.

- You could be told that you have the qualifications and training which, prima facie, meet the requirements for eligibility for AIR membership. However, you may need twelve months' clinical supervision when you arrive in Australia.

- You may be told that you do not reach the required standard but that you could possibly reach it by completing successfully an accredited bridging course conducted by a recognised college in Australia.

- You could be advised that you are well below the standard and you would need to complete successfully a retraining program in Australia before you would be considered for institute membership.

The minimum academic standard is used as a basis for assessment but other factors, such as the type of your course, will also be considered. Your recent experience must be broadly based and include basic experience in one or more forms of digital imaging.

- If you graduated since 1986, you must have had at least two years' full-time practical experience within five years of the consideration of your application.

- If you graduated between 1976 and 1985, you must have had three years' full-time experience in the five years before consideration of your application.

- If you graduated in 1975 or earlier and you have had many years of virtually uninterrupted radiographic experience including the five years before consideration of your application, then your case will be considered on its merits.

For further information contact NOOSR or AIR.

### Social Welfare

Australian social work courses require at least four years of education at tertiary institutions which award a Bachelor degree as the basic social work qualification. The **Australian Association of Social Workers** (AASW) requires at least four years of degree-level, full-time study or its part-time equivalent for association membership. This study must lead to a distinct qualification in social work.

The assessment of an overseas qualification is based on how it compares with an Australian social work program. If your qualification is assessed at a three-year degree level of Australian study you can take a one-year course at an Australian university to bridge the gap. There is a shorter supplementary course if your needs are in field work only. These programs are arranged through the AASW.

For further information about how your social work qualifications will be assessed contact NOOSR or: The Australian Association of Social Workers, PO Box 84, Hawker, ACT 2614. Qualified welfare workers should contact: The Australian Institute of Welfare and Community Workers, GPO Box 2557, Canberra, ACT 2601.

## Teaching

Teachers who have been trained overseas and want to work in Australia must have tertiary teaching qualifications comparable to those offered by Australian universities. Not only this, but you will also have to adapt to different teaching traditions, a different educational structure and a different organisational system.

Many overseas teaching qualifications are generally acceptable in Australia but the authorities do not automatically recognise particular qualifications. All qualifications are assessed on how they compare with Australian teacher education standards.

If your qualifications are accepted by a registration board or employing authority this does not guarantee that you will find a teaching post. This will depend on a number of other factors including job availability and your own suitability for a particular post. If you are accepted in one state or territory this does not mean that you will be automatically accepted in another as each has its own requirements.

Registration or employing authorities usually require teachers from abroad to have completed a course of teacher education equivalent to an Australian course.

If you wish to migrate to Australia as a teacher your qualifications must meet the criteria of the government school system in at least one state or territory. If you want an assessment of your qualifications for migration purposes then you should read the *Procedures Advice Manual* published by the Department of Immigration, Local Government and Ethnic Affairs, available at all of the offices of that Department in Australia or overseas. It gives valuable information on the overseas teaching qualifications which can be assessed by migration officers. Other qualifications are assessed by NOOSR.

If you are applying for assessment to NOOSR then you will need to supply the following documents: Form 44 — the Application for

Assessment of Professional, Para-professional or Technical Skills and Qualifications, available from all migration offices; certified copies of — original award certificates for all qualifications, original transcripts of mark sheets listing all subjects studied and grades awarded and any details of supervised teaching practice, the letter from the Australian migration authorities requesting that you have your application assessed; and the fee advised by the migration officer.

Once you arrive in Australia you can apply for registration and/or employment with the following authorities:

*New South Wales*
Department of School Education, PO Box 6000, Parramatta, NSW 2124.

*Victoria*
Government schools: Teachers' Registration Board, 49-51 Spring Street, Melbourne, Victoria 3000. Non-government schools: Registered Schools Board, Rialto Tower, 525 Collins Street, Melbourne, Victoria 3001.

*Queensland*
Board of Teacher Registration. PO Box 389, Toowong, Queensland 4066.

*South Australia*
Teachers' Registration Board, 1st Floor, 45 Wakefield Street, Adelaide, South Australia.

*Western Australia*
Human Resources Services Branch, Ministry of Education, 151 Royal Street, East Perth, Western Australia 6000.

*Tasmania*
Government schools: Department of Education, GPO Box 169B, Hobart, Tasmania 7001. Non-government schools: Teachers and Schools Registration Board, GPO Box 169B, Hobart, Tasmania 7001.

*Australian Capital Territory*
Teaching Service Section, Ministry for Health, Education and the Arts, PO Box 20, Civic Square, ACT 2608.

*Northern Territory*
Personnel Branch, NT Department of Education, PO Box 4821, Darwin, Northern Territory 0801.

## Technicians

The profession of technician in Australia covers medical technical officers and technicians, science technical officers and technicians, electrical and electronic engineering associates and technicians, mechanical engineering associates and technicians, building, architectural and surveying associates and technicians.

Overseas qualifications for technicians are assessed against the requirements for obtaining an appropriate award from one of the Australian TAFE colleges. NOOSR assessments are available to the following categories:

● Prospective migrants who have been advised by an Australian diplomatic mission to seek assessment of their qualifications.

● Overseas-trained people who are already living in Australia and want their qualifications assessed for employment.

When you apply for migration you will be told which documents are required for assessment of your qualifications and skills. The fee for assessment by NOOSR in this field is $A100.

## Veterinary Science

All veterinarians in Australia must be registered with a veterinary surgeon's board before they can practise. Bachelor degrees from United Kingdom universities are acceptable but if you gained your degree from the University of Dublin or the University of Ireland then you should contact the registrar of the veterinary surgeon's board in the state or territory where you wish to practise. If you graduated from any other university then you will be required to sit the National Veterinary Examination.

For further information contact: The Executive Officer, Panel in Veterinary Science, NOOSR, PO Box 1407, Canberra, ACT 2601.

Veterinarians with qualifications from United Kingdom universities who are eligible for immediate registration in Australia should contact the Registrars in the relevant states and territories:

*New South Wales*
Board of Veterinary Surgeons of New South Wales, PO Box K220, Haymarket, NSW 2000.

*Queensland*
Veterinary Surgeons' Board of Queensland, c/o Department of Primary Industries, GPO Box 46, Brisbane, Queensland 4001.

*South Australia*
Veterinary Surgeons' Board of South Australia, GPO Box 1671, Adelaide, South Australia 5001.

*Western Australia*
Veterinary Surgeons' Board of Western Australia, 28 Charles Street, South Perth, Western Australia 6151.

*Tasmania*
Veterinary Board of Tasmania, GPO Box 192B, Hobart, Tasmania 7001.

*Australian Capital Territory*
Veterinary Surgeon's Board of the Australian Capital Territory, GPO Box 825, Canberra, ACT 2601.

*Northern Territory*
Veterinary Surgeon's Board of the Northern Territory, PO Box 4160, Darwin, Northern Territory 5794.

*Victoria*
Veterinary Board of Victoria, 272 Brunswick Road, Brunswick, Victoria 3056.

## RECOGNITION OF TRADE SKILLS

The metal and electrical trades have a system by which overseas-trained tradespeople can have their qualifications recognised in Australia. This is done by obtaining an **Australian Recognised Tradesman's Certificate**. This can only be issued if you permanently reside in Australia, but eligibility for recognition can be assessed prior to migration. The certificates are issued under the Tradesmen's Rights Regulation Act 1946, and the term tradesman applies to both male and female workers.

The trades covered by the act covers five groups: engineering, boilermaking, sheetmetal, blacksmithing and electrical. The overall policy for determining the conditions under which a person is assessed is laid down by Central Trades Committees for each of these five groups. Local Trades Committees determine individual applications and issue Australian Recognised Tradesman's Certificates to persons who meet the requirements.

You may be eligible for an Australian Recognised Tradesman's Certificate if you have completed trade training outside Australia and/or have worked as a tradesperson overseas for specified periods in a recognised trade, and:

● your training and employment is assessed as equivalent to that of an Australian apprenticeship, or

● you have gained an acceptable standard and range of skills with, subsequently, six years employment on work ordinarily performed by a tradesperson in any one of the listed metal trades, or seven years employment on work ordinarily performed by a tradesperson in any one of the listed electrical trades. You must also be capable of doing the work of the relevant trade in Australia.

## Definition of 'tradesman'

The Central Trades Committee defines a tradesman as a broadly trained and/or experienced tradesperson who has gained, as a minimum, sufficient knowledge and skills to:

● read working instructions and technical drawings common to his or her trade;

● plan independently the method and order of progressing a job;

● take measurements and readings using measuring instruments of appropriate accuracy;

● mark out, lay out and set up trade work;

● select appropriate materials, tools, machines and/or equipment;

● make appropriate settings on tools, machines and/or equipment;

● carry out trade work independently;

● check and/or test trade work in relation to the standards applying to his or her trade.

When you apply to have your trade qualifications assessed you should initially contact your nearest Australian High Commission,

Consulate or Embassy. You may need to have them assessed before being permitted to migrate but even if this is not the case it is a good idea to get an assessment so that you can estimate your chances of recognition when you arrive in Australia.

## How to get a Trade Test

Once you are in Australia you will need to satisfy a Local Trades Committee that you meet the requirements to be issued with an Australian Recognised Tradesman's Certificate. In order to do this you can undertake a **Trade Test** when you get to Australia. For this you will need the following documents:

- evidence of your identity and age;

- evidence of completion of your technical and vocational education, including final certificates or diplomas, and the details of the duration of the course and subjects passed;

- evidence of completion of any trade or trade-related courses, including final certificates or diplomas;

- evidence of completion of your apprenticeship or traineeship, including contracts of apprenticeship or traineeship and final certificates or diplomas, and details of the main parts of the training program and their duration;

- evidence of your trade or trade-related employment, from all your previous employers. (This should be a statement of service on the official letterhead paper of your employers, without any alterations or erasures, and signed by an identifiable senior member of the firm's management. The statement must show trade classification or classifications in which you were employed, period of employment, including exact dates in each classification, and a detailed description of your training. It is not necessary to obtain a statement of service from your present employer, if this would cause problems in your present job.);

- evidence of trade or trade-related self-employment, such as: a personal statement on a properly signed statutory declaration providing details of the exact commencement and completion dates of business, classification in which you were self-employed, number of staff employed and their classifications, and a full description of work, tools and equipment used; Certificate of Business Registration covering each year of self-employment; statement on letterhead paper from your accountant or legal representative certifying the name and nature of your business, the exact dates and period of self-employment and the capacity in which you were self-employed, statements from suppliers confirming the nature of your business and dates of trading period; and statements from clients, on letterhead paper, confirming full details of the work you performed for them and dates and periods worked;

● evidence of trade training and/or employment in the Defence Forces, including discharge certificate if applicable;

● evidence of licensing or registration.

If you cannot obtain some of the required documents, your application may still be considered if you submit a statutory declaration giving the reasons why evidence is unobtainable.

## Trades
The following are the trades covered by the Tradesmen's Rights Regulation Act, and which require an Australian Recognised Tradesman's Certificate.

*Engineering*
Adjuster
Coppersmith
Electroplater, first class
First class machinist (Boring)
First class machinist (Drilling)
First class machinist (Grinding)
First class machinist (Milling)
First class welder (Engineering)
Fitter (Diesel)
Fitter and first class machinist
Fitter
Fitter (Instruments)
Fitter and turner
Ground engineer (Airframe)
Ground engineer (Engines)
Ground engineer (Airframes and Engines)

Ground engineer (Instruments)
Locksmith
Machine setter
Mechanic (Marine and other Engines), excluding persons engaged solely
    on maintaining motors of less than 200cc capacity
Motor cycle mechanic
Pattern maker
Refrigeration mechanic or serviceman
Repairer (Security work)
Scalemaker
Scalemaker and adjuster
Scientific instrument maker
Turner

*Boilermaker*
Angle-ironsmith
Boilermaker
Boilermaker and structural steel tradesman
Marker-off (a tradesman, the greater part of whose time is occupied in
    marking-off or template making, or both)
Structural steel tradesman
Welder, first class

*Blacksmithing*
Angle-ironsmith
Annealer
Annealer and case hardener
Blacksmith
Case hardener
First class welder (Smithing)
Forger
Smith, other
Toolsmith
Tradesman heat treater

*Sheetmetal*
Body maker, first class
First class welder
Panel beater
Sheetmetal worker, first class

*Electrical trades*
Armature winder
Armature winder (Automotive)
Electrical fitter
Electrical fitter (Automotive)
Electrical fitter and armature winder
Electrical fitter and armature winder (Automotive)
Electrical fitter (Instruments)
Electrical mechanic
Ground engineer (Electrical)
Ground engineer (Instruments)
Ground engineer (Radio)
Refrigeration mechanic or serviceman
Telegraph mechanic
Tradesman (Radio)
Tradesman (Television)
Tradesman (Radio and Television)

## OFFICES OF LOCAL TRADES COMMITTEES

*New South Wales (including ACT)*
10th Floor, 255 Pitt Street, Sydney, NSW 2000. Postal address GPO Box 9879, Sydney, NSW 2001.

*Victoria*
13th Floor Rialto Building North Tower, 525 Collins Street, Melbourne, VIC 3000. Postal address GPO Box 9879, Melbourne, VIC 3001.

*Queensland*
11th Floor, 127 Creek Street, Brisbane, QLD 4000. Postal address GPO Box 9879, Brisbane, QLD 4001.

*Western Australia*
8th Floor, 190 St. Georges Terrace, Perth, WA 6000. Postal address GPO Box 9879, Perth, WA 6001.

*South Australia*
Mezzanine Floor, Hooker House, 33 King William Street, Adelaide, SA 5000. Postal address GPO Box 9879, Adelaide, SA 5001.

*Tasmania*
Level 6, Stock Exchange Building, 83-85 Macquarie Street, Hobart, TAS 7000. Postal address GPO Box 9879, Hobart, TAS 7001.

*Northern Territory*
Kriewaldt Chambers, 6 Searcy Street, Darwin, NT 0800. Postal address GPO Box 9879, Darwin, NT 0801.

# 10

## Vocational Training

### DEPARTMENT OF EDUCATION, TRAINING AND YOUTH AFFAIRS (DETYA)

The Department of Education, Training and Youth Affairs (DETYA) offers a wide range of services covering a variety of employment and training issues. Much of this information is now readily available on the Internet and two useful addresses are:

- http:/www.detya.gov.au/JobGuideOnline. which gives education and training details for more than 400 jobs in Australia, as well as addresses for TAFE colleges and CES addresses.

- http:/www.detya.gov.au/pubs/pubs.htm which gives full details of the extensive services offered by DETYA.

If you prefer to use the old fashioned method and obtain written information the address is: Department of Education, Training and Youth Affairs, 16–18 Mort Street, GPO Box 9880, Canberra ACT 2601. Tel: (06) 240 8111.

### TECHNICAL AND FURTHER EDUCATION (TAFE)

The network of Technical and Further Education (TAFE) colleges throughout Australia are the main means for vocational training in the country. They provide an enormous variety of courses which are aimed at providing training for a specific job or vocational area. There are over 1200 different courses which can be taken at over 1000 colleges and associated centres in Australia.

TAFE colleges offer three main qualifications:

1. **Diploma Courses**. These usually consist of three years of full-time study or five years of part-time study.

2.  **Associate Diploma Courses**. These usually consist of two years of full-time study or four years of part-time study.

3.  **Advanced Certificate Courses**. These are courses which lead to state registered awards — endorsements, statements of attainment and college statements. Endorsements are granted for courses which follow on from another specified TAFE course.

On completion of one TAFE course you can then progress to a higher-level course within the TAFE system.

## Special entry requirements

Although TAFE courses are generally geared towards school-leavers and students they are available to anyone. Special admission can be granted to people over 20 years old who do not have the necessary entry requirements for a specific course but who can show evidence of a suitable educational background and/or abilities gained in occupational or life experience.

## The TAFE year

The period of study at TAFE colleges is divided into four terms, roughly equivalent to those in the public school system. Some courses follow a semester pattern; two semesters per year, each of 18 weeks, with a break of one or two weeks in the middle. Most courses begin in February but some start in July.

Due to the fact that many people who attend TAFE colleges are already employed it is possible to take a number of part-time courses at night. Fees for Diploma and Associate Diploma courses are approximately $A30 per year. You may also have to pay for books, tools and any other equipment which you will need.

For anyone who is thinking of undertaking vocational training in an attempt to improve their job prospects in Australia then TAFE is an invaluable service.

For more information about TAFE in each state or territory contact:

*Australian Capital Territory*
ACT Institute of TAFE, PO Box 826, Canberra City, ACT 2601.

*New South Wales*
TAFE Information Centre, 849 George Street, Railway Square, Broadway, NSW 2007.

*Northern Territory*
TAFE Division, Northern Territory Division Department of Education, 69 Smith Street, Darwin, NT 0800.

*Queensland*
TAFE Information Centre, PO Box 33, North Quay, QLD 4002.

*South Australia*
TAFE Information Centre, Education Centre, 31 Flinders Street, Adelaide, SA 5000.

*Tasmania*
Hobart Technical College, 75 Campbell Street, Hobart, TAS 7000.

*Victoria*
Vocational Orientation Centre, 328 Queen Street, Melbourne, VIC 3000.

*Western Australia*
TAFE Information Centre, WA Department of Education, Cable House, Victoria Avenue, Perth, WA 6000.

## UNIVERSITIES

Most Australian universities and colleges offer a range of vocational courses. The range of qualifications offered in most cases are degrees, diplomas, associate diplomas, transfer courses, postgraduate courses and conversion courses. The following is a selection of universities who place particular emphasis on vocational subjects.

### New South Wales and ACT
Australian National University, Canberra Institute of Arts, GPO Box 4, Canberra, ACT. Tel: 06 249 5111.

Charles Sturt University, Private Mailbag 7, Bathurst 2795. Tel: 063 31 1022.

Macquarie University, Balaclava Road, North Ryde 2113. Tel: 02 805 7111.

University of New England, Armidale 2351. Tel: 067 73 333.

University of New South Wales, Anzac Parade, Kensington 2033. PO Box 1. Tel: 02 697 2222.

University of Newcastle, McMullan Building, Rankin Drive, Shortland 2308. Tel: 049 68 0401.

University of Sydney, Science Road, University of Sydney 2006. Tel: 02 692 2222.

University of Technology, Sydney, Broadway Campus, 15-73 Broadway 2007. PO Box 123. Tel: 02 20 930.

University of Wollongong, Northfields Avenue, North Wollongong 2500. PO Box 1144. Tel: 042 27 0555.

## Victoria

Ballarat University College, PO Box 663, Ballarat 3350. Tel: 053 33 9000.

Deakin University, Pigdons Road, Geelong 3217. Tel 052 47 1111.

La Trobe University, Bubdoora 3083. Tel: 03 479 1111.

Monash University, Wellington Road, Clayton 3168. Tel: 03 565 4000.

Philip Institute of Technology, PO Box 179, Coburg 3058. Tel: 03 353 9222.

Swinburne Institute of Technology, Box 218, Hawthorn 3122. Tel: 03 819 8911.

University of Melbourne, Parkville 3052. Tel: 03 344 4000.

Victoria College, 221 Burwood Highway, Burwood 3125. Tel: 03 285 3333.

Victoria University of Technology, GPO Box 2476V, Melbourne 3001. Tel: 03 662 0611.

## Queensland

Griffith University, (including Gold Coast University College), Kessels Road, Nathan 4111. Tel: 07 875 7111.

James Cook University of North Queensland, Townsville 4811. Tel: 077 81 4111.

Queensland University of Technology, GPO Box 2434, Brisbane 4001. Tel: 07 223 2111.

University of Queensland, Queensland Agricultural College, St. Lucia 4067. Tel: 07 377 1111.

Bond University, Private Bag 10, Gold Cost Mail Centre 4217.

## South Australia

Flinders University of South Australia, Sturt Campus, Sturt Road, Bedford Park 5042. Tel: 08 275 3911.

University of Adelaide, GPO Box 498, Adelaide 5001. Tel: 08 228 5333.

University of South Australia, North Terrace, Adelaide 5000. Tel: 08 236 2211.

## Western Australia

Curtain University of Technology, Kent Street, Bentley 6012. Tel: 09 351 1466.

Murdoch University, South Street, Murdoch 6150. Tel: 09 332 2421.
University of Western Australia, Nedlands 6009. Tel: 09 380 3050.
Edith Cowan University, Person Street, Churchlands 6018. Tel: 09 383 8333.

### Tasmania
University of Tasmania, GPO Box 252C, Hobart 7001. Tel: 002 20 2101.

### Northern Territory
Northern Territory University, PO Box 40146. Casuarina 0811. Tel: 089
46 6666.

### Adult entry
Most of the above universities operate special adult entry admission
schemes whereby people over a certain age are admitted on the basis of
work experience and qualifications other than purely academic ones.
The universities which are most likely to offer this type of entry are:
University of Technology Sydney, University of Sydney, University of
New South Wales, Curtain University of Technology, University of New
England, Queensland University, Edith Cowan University, Macquarie
University and University of South Australia.

### Part-time
The following are the biggest providers of part-time education:
University of Technology Sydney, University of Sydney, University of
New South Wales, Curtain University of Technology, University of New
England, Queensland University, Victoria University of Technology,
Melbourne University, Queensland University of Technology, Edith
Cowan University, Macquarie University, La Trobe University and
University of South Australia.

## GOVERNMENT VOCATIONAL SCHEMES

Through the Department of Employment, Workplace Relations and
Small Business, the Federal Government is very aware of the need to
give unemployed people a chance to get back into the workforce. There
are a number of schemes intended to do this.

### Jobstart
This is a scheme which offers employers subsidies to employ long-term
unemployed of all ages. To qualify you have to have been unemployed
for six months in the last nine months. If Centrelink thinks that you are

particularly disadvantaged then this may be waived. Wage subsidies range from $50 to $320 depending on the award rate for the job and the age of the applicant. The employer has to pay the current award rate of pay so they cannot cut corners as far as the employee is concerned.

## JobTraining
This provides vocational training for people of all ages through established and specially created courses. The same eligibility conditions as for JobStart apply.

## Innovate training: Projects-National skills
These are projects designed to target skill shortages in specific area that are having an adverse effect on the economy. Once this has been done short-term training is given in these areas. In recent years this has included the following programs:

- National Skills Shortages.
- Labour Adjustment Programs.
- Heavy Engineering Adjustment and Development Programs.
- Textile, Clothing and Footwear Labour Adjustment programs.

These not only provide updated training for people who have been working in these industries but, perhaps more importantly for migrants from Britain, they act as bridging courses for qualified workers from overseas seeking to make their qualifications acceptable to the Australian employment market. There are also programs to upgrade the skills of existing workers.

## Job Search Training Program
This program is designed to give unemployed people all the assistance they need for finding work and to equip them with the necessary job-finding skills. These are two main schemes within the program:

*1. Job Search Training Courses*
These are courses given by local community and educational groups that run for a total of twenty-two hours. Applicants must be:

- registered unemployed;
- have an idea of what they want to do;
- possess the necessary skills, qualifications and experience for the

job they are seeking;
- be prepared to take an active part in the training program;
- able to speak, read and write English.

The course covers various aspects of job-hunting including: filling in application forms, writing letters of application and CVs, telephoning employers and interview technique.

*2. Job Clubs*
This is a longer program — three weeks — which is intended to give the long-term unemployed and special groups such as single parents and the disabled the necessary job-seeking skills. The course consists of a combination of theory and practice and those on it have access to everything they need for applying for jobs: postage, stationery, telephones, photocopiers, and typewriters.

## The Australian Traineeship System
This is a new form of vocational training for young people aged between sixteen and nineteen. It is designed to help young people find vocational employment and also bring benefits to industry by providing them with well trained staff. The system has been designed through consultation between employers, trade unions, the education sector, trainers and young people themselves.

Trainees of the scheme receive twelve months of quality training in non-trade occupations. This is made up of on-the-job training and also practical study at TAFE colleges or approved training centres. The training includes:

- job specific training in a range of occupational skills
- training in general skills such as numeracy
- the development of personal work effectiveness skills.

Trainees who complete the course satisfactorily receive a certificate from the State/Territory Training Authority, which is recognised nationally.

Some of the traineeships currently on offer are: Australian Public Service, automotive, banking, business equipment maintenance, clerk — legal office, computer programming, electrical goods manufacturing, financial services, food service assistant, furniture removals, insurance, local government, office skills, plastics, retails sales assistant, rural, small offset printing, software support, textiles and clothing, timber merchandising and travel industry.

## APPRENTICESHIPS

Apprenticeships are widespread in Australian trades and there are two main types:

1. **Indentured** — where an agreement is signed by the apprentice and the employer.
2. **Trainee** — no agreement is signed and there is no guarantee of continued employment.

Apprentices have to be at least 15 years old and they can complete an apprenticeship technical training course by:

- day release;
- block study;
- external study.

Most apprenticeships last four years but some can be shorter.

# 11

# Applying for Work

Although the basics of applying for a job in Australia are essentially the same as in the UK the main point to remember is that the Australian character is slightly different to its British counterpart. The lack of class barriers means that Australians are more interested in whether you are able to do the job, than in what school or university you went to. Also, pretension and affectation will be given short shrift — down-to-earth honesty and straightforwardness are the orders of the day.

## HOW TO APPLY

When making written applications for a job, whether it is on a speculative basis or on an official application form, it pays to be:

- precise;
- positive;
- honest.

Australians are not great ones for waffle and padding. They are more interested in one short sentence coming straight to the point rather than two paragraphs skirting around the issue. They also like to see an upbeat, positive attitude. Don't say things like, 'I was not very good as a manager in Britain but I hope to get better.' Instead say, 'In the present economic climate I feel I have a variety of skills to offer, which will greatly benefit your business.' Then go on to list those skills, but again, briefly.

Some people think that it is permissible to be economical with the truth on job application forms. This may be true in that some things will never be checked. However, if it is something that is important for the job then sooner or later you will be found out. If it is not important then it is not worth lying about in the first place. Australians set great store by honesty and a solid, reliable worker is often preferred to a well-qualified but shady one.

## HANDLING YOUR INTERVIEW

The rules for applications apply just the same for interviews, as do the normal things you would do for an interview in Britain:

- Be well dressed.
- Have clean and tidy hair.
- Be punctual.
- Find out the name of your interviewer if possible and use it.
- Find out as much as possible about the company to which you are applying.
- Do not fidget or move around unnecessarily during the interview.
- Have proof of your qualifications.
- Be prepared to ask questions.
- Do not tell other interviewees what questions you were asked.

### Dress

The main differences will come from the novelty of a different environment and culture. The first difference will be in your attire for the interview. At home you would probably wear something respectable and non-descript — the safe option. But you should dress appropriately for your environment. If you are in Sydney or Melbourne in the middle of winter then this may be similar to Britain and so the safe option would be in order. However, if you were in Brisbane at the height of summer or further north in the sub-tropical belt of Australia then a grey suit may look slightly incongruous. This is not to suggest that you should turn up in a beach shirt and thongs (flip-flops) but a certain relaxation of the normal interview wear could be allowed. To get an idea of what would be acceptable take a look around and see what people in the profession you are applying to are wearing. Follow suit, literally.

### Attitudes

The second difference in the interview may be the attitude of your interviewer. He or she will want to find out what kind of a person you are, not the cut of your school tie. Questions may be direct and to the point and answers should be in a similar vein, but try not to be too blunt.

One important consideration for interviews is to avoid being too critical. This applies particularly to the country you have come from; you will not ingratiate yourself to your interviewer by declaring, 'Britain is such a dump, I'm glad I got away.' Contrary to popular belief Australians do not dislike Poms as they would like to pretend, but they are opposed to 'whinging' of any kind. They will not be inclined to employ people who come across as negative.

## THE AUSTRALIAN WAY OF WORK

Three of the most commonly used colloquialisms in the Australian workplace are, 'sickie', 'bludger' and 'dobber'.

- The **sickie** is a piece of wonderful Australian logic which reasons that since there is an allowance for you to take a certain numbers of days off a year through sickness that you should take them whether you are actually ill or not. Perhaps they are just putting into words what goes unsaid in other countries but the sickie is as much a part of the Australian workplace as income tax or overtime payments. Whether you conform to the sickie philosophy or not is a personal choice, but when in Rome. . .

- A **bludger** is someone who is lazy and does not do their job properly. It is often used as a playful term of abuse and should not be taken too seriously. However, if your employer begins to think of you as a bludger then this could have an adverse effect on your prospects. It is better to get known for doing 'hard yakka' rather than for being a bludger. Hard yakka is a term for hard work or hard graft.

- A **dobber** is a much more serious offender in the workplace. In effect it is a grass who goes to the boss to tell tales on his fellow workmates. Australian workers have very strong bonds of solidarity and if anyone breaks the unspoken code that all workers stick together come what may they will be treated at best with silence and at worst with violence.

### Means to an end

In many ways Australians have a good attitude to their jobs in the overall scheme of things: it is a task to be taken seriously but it should not be allowed to take over your life. However, the attitudes vary in different professions. In 1991 the Australian Bureau of Statistics published a survey which showed that 1.3 million Australians worked more than 49 hours a week. Most of these were managers and administrators. Professionals averaged 37 hours a week while labourers and those in related work clocked in at an average of 31 hours a week. If you are prepared to accept an honest wage for an honest week's work then, as they say, 'She'll be right, mate!'

Australians like to socialise after a hard day at the office/factory/-kitchen/vineyard and they invariably do this with their workmates. This is not just a case of a few tinnies of Fosters after work; they will invite you to barbecues at their home or to a day at the beach at the weekend. This type of invitation should be treated exactly as it is intended — an open gesture of friendship. Australians are not hung up on workplace hierarchy and once it is time to go home then everyone is very much an equal.

## Mateship

Depending on your point of view, the concept of Australian mateship is either an example of an unique form of male bonding, or an outdated example of extreme macho chauvinism. It is prevalent in all aspects of Australian society and the workplace is no exception. Thankfully though mateship seems to be on the decline as Australian men begin to realise that friendship does not have revolve exclusively around swill tubes of Fosters and sticking up for your mate no matter what he has done.

You may be confronted by mateship on two levels: aimed against migrants and women. As a migrant you will be accepted happily enough into the workplace but there may be some elements who are not prepared to trust you fully until you have proved your true worth in the mateship stakes (what this involves is a mystery to those not initiated into the inner circle but is has been rumoured that this involves surviving forty days and forty nights in the outback or drinking a tanker of Castlemaine XXXX in one go).

The overcoming of mateship from a female perspective is slightly harder. First you will have to prove that you are as good as the mateship fraternity, then prove you are better, and then be prepared to let them take the limelight. Whatever you do make sure that you are not intimidated by mateship — the mateship brigade admires spirit and boldness as much as anything else.

The concept of mateship may seem somewhat archaic in the 1990s and its impact is definitely lessening in the workplace. However, it must be remembered that this is a society that until the 1950s banned women from drinking in the majority of its pubs. The baser side of mateship may be dying, but it is not dead.

## CHECKLIST FOR THE AUSTRALIAN WORKPLACE

1. Although working in Australia can be similar to Britain in many ways there are subtle differences in style, approach and attitudes.

2.  Be positive and upbeat but not showy or pushy.

3.  Concentrate on your future rather than dwell on your past achievements, or otherwise.

4.  Be prepared to listen and learn — do not say things like, 'Back home we used to do it this way. . .'

5.  You will be rewarded for reliable, hard work so try and capitalise on this.

6.  Do not criticise people for taking sickies — it is as much a part of Australian life as Fosters and Paul Hogan.

7.  You may get away with being a bludger but definitely not a dobber.

8.  Enjoy your job but make sure you take advantage of your life outside the workplace.

9.  Accept the fact that mateship exists in the workplace but try not to get involved.

10. Hope Australia wins as many major sporting events as possible — when Alan Bond won the America's Cup Bob Hawke announced a public holiday the following day.

# 12

## Casual Work Opportunities

Not all people who are looking for work in Australia are intending to migrate there and find permanent jobs. Young people arriving Down Under with holiday working visas are more interested in short-term casual employment, to supplement their travels.

As with migrant employment the casual job market has been hit by the recession and there is no longer any guarantee that you will be able to get a job within five minutes of walking off the plane. Although some industries, such as catering, have been particularly hard hit the casual job-seeker can, with a certain amount of dedication and hard work, spend a profitable year working around Australia.

## THE JOB SEARCH

### Centrelink
As with permanent employees, people with holiday working visas can take advantage of the Centrelink Customer Services Centres around the country. They will be able to give job hunter's advice on catering, fruit picking and labouring, or direct you to the areas where the workers are most needed. See page 59 for a list of the Centrelink offices around the country or visit their Web site at: www.centrelink.gov.au/ Alternatively look at the government Web site, JobSearch, for current employment vacancies, at: www.jobsearch.gov.au/

### Private agencies
The private employment agencies are worth considering for people looking for temporary employment, particularly in secretarial and clerical work. There are also agencies which specialise in placing casual workers for jobs such as cleaning and gardening. If you are going to be stationed in one place for a reasonable period of time then you will have a better chance to get established with an agency and provide yourself with a steady stream of temporary work.

All major agencies advertise in the local *Yellow Pages* and a selection of them are listed elsewhere in this book.

## Opportunism

Sometimes the best way to find casual employment is to keep your eyes open, your ears close to the ground and all other parts of your body in a state of readiness. Look for private advertisements in shop windows or youth hostels noticeboards, or ask fellow travellers for tips about the job market in areas they have visited.

Being the straightforward people that Australians are, sometimes the best way to find job leads is to go into the nearest pub, sit yourself down with a drink and see what happens. This may sound like advice from a brewery PR man but it could be a good investment to buy a few drinks and get chatting with the locals. You may not be offered a job there and then but you may well gain some local knowledge that will point you in the right direction.

It can also pay to promote your own talents. Put notices in local shops offering to cut lawns, paint walls or dig ditches. Alternatively go door-to-door offering your services for any odd-jobs that might need to be done. Even if you do not get snowed under with work you will undoubtedly have some interesting experiences doing this. Another method would be to put an advertisement in a local newspaper. Perhaps something along the lines of: 'Willing worker seeking serious employment in the odd-job business. Nothing is too big, too small or too ludicrous. Years of experience in several continents. Competitive rates that will not break the mortgage.' If this does not work in one area then try it somewhere else where people are more understanding.

## FRUIT PICKING

This is traditionally a boom area for casual employment. Not only that, but it is a good way for the overseas worker to see a side of Australian life which they would not see in a big city. The work is hard and dirty and the financial rewards vary from the mediocre to the excellent. To find fruit picking work you should go to the Centrelink office nearest to the area in which you want to work. They will advise you on job availability. Due to problems in other sectors of the economy more and more people are now turning to fruit-picking for a living. This means there are less places for casual workers from abroad. This at least is the official line you will hear from the Centrelink. Unofficially, the nature of fruit-picking and the poor conditions under which the workers live means that pickers are frequently walking off the job. The best way to land a picking job is to go to a fruit growing area and start knocking on a few farm doors. People have even been approached on the street in fruit picking towns and offered jobs. The best time is towards the end of the season when the growers are getting desperate to get their crops in and the pickers are getting fed up with their task.

Fruit picking as a means of employment during a year in Australia is not only a good idea from the financial point-of-view, it also has the big advantage of being the type of work that you would not come across at home. Making use of a holiday working visa is not so much about how much you earn but rather what you do. Fruit picking will be an experience you will never forget, no matter how hard you try.

## Harvest times and areas

*New South Wales*

| Harvest period | Crop | Area | Nearest Agency |
|---|---|---|---|
| Jan | Apricot, prunes and peaches | Griffith | Griffith |
| Feb-Mar | Prunes | Young | Young |
| | Grapes | Griffith | Griffith |
| | | Leeton | Leeton |
| | Cherries | Forbes | Parkes |
| | Peaches | Forbes | Parkes |
| Feb-Apr | Apples | Oranges | Oranges |
| | Pears | Forbes | Parkes |
| Feb-May | Apples | Forbes | Parkes |
| Mar-Apr | Apples | Batlow | Tumut |
| | Beans | Forbes | Parkes |
| | Zucchinis | Forbes | Parkes |
| | Peas | Forbes | Parkes |
| Mar-June | Cotton | Wee Waa | Narrabri |
| Sep-Apr | Oranges | Griffith | Griffith |
| Sep-Dec | Asparagus | Dubbo | Dubbo |
| Oct-Dec | Asparagus | CowraCowra Forbes | Parkes |
| Nov-Dec | Cherries | Young | Young |

| Harvest period | Crop | Area | Nearest Agency |
|---|---|---|---|
| Nov-Jan | Cotton chipping | Wee Waa | Narrabri |
| | Cherries | Oranges | Oranges |
| Nov-Feb | Cotton chipping | Moree | Moree |
| Nov-Mar | Onions | Griffith | Griffith |
| Nov-Apr | Tomatoes | Forbes | Parkes |
| Dec-Mar | Oranges | Leeton | Leeton |

*Victoria*

| Harvest period | Crop | Area | Nearest Agency |
|---|---|---|---|
| Jan-Mar | Pears, peaches | Shepparton | Shepparton |
| | | Ardmona | Shepparton |
| | | Tatura | Shepparton |
| | | Kyabram | Kyabram |
| | | Invergordon | Kyabram |
| | | Cobram | Cobram |
| Jan-Apr | Table grapes | Sunraysia | Mildura |
| | | Robinvale | Mildura |
| Feb-Apr | Tomatoes | Shepparton | Shepparton |
| | | Ardmona | Shepparton |
| | | Tatura | Shepparton |
| | | Kyabram | Kyabram |
| | | Echuca and | |
| | | Tongala | Echuca |
| | | Rochester | Rochester |
| Feb-Mar | Grapes | Nyah District | |
| | | Swan Hill | Swan Hill |
| | | Lake Boga | Swan Hill |
| | | Robinvale | Robinvale |
| | | Sunraysia | Mildura |
| Jan-Apr | Tobacco | Ovens, King Wangaratta and Kiewa Valleys | |
| Mar-Apr | Apples | Red Hill | Rosebud |
| | | Main Bridge | Rosebud |
| Sep-Nov | Asparagus | Dalmore | Dandenong |

| Harvest period | Crop | Area | Nearest Agency |
|---|---|---|---|
| Oct-Dec | Strawberries | Echuca<br>Kyabram<br>Silvan | Echuca<br>Kyabram<br>Lilydale |
| Nov-Feb | Cherries and berries | Wandin<br>Silvan<br>Healesville | Lilydale<br>Lilydale<br>Lilydale |
| Nov-Dec | Tomato weeding | Echuca<br>Rochester<br>Tongala | Echuca<br>Echuca<br>Echuca |
| *Queensland*<br>Jan-Feb | Grapes | Stanthorpe | Warwick |
| Feb-Mar | Pears | Stanthorpe | Warwick |
| Feb-Mar | Apples | Stanthorpe | Warwick |
| Mar-Apr | Ginger | Nambour | Nambour |
| Apr-Nov | Beans | Mary Valley | Gympie |
| May-Dec | Sugar cane | Ingham<br>Innisfail | Ingham<br>Innisfail |
| May-Dec | Small crops | Ayr | Ayr |
| Jul-Sep | Ginger | Nambour | Nambour |
| Jul-Oct | Strawberries | Nambour | Nambour |
| Aug-Dec | Asparagus | Warwick | Warwick |
| Aug-Nov | Small crops | Ayr | Ayr |
| Sep-Nov | Potatoes/onions | Lockyer Valley | Toowoomba<br>Gatton |
| Sep-Nov | Tobacco | Mareeba | Mareeba |
| Oct-Dec | Tomatoes | Bundaberg | Bundaberg |
| Dec | Stone fruits | Stanthorpe | Warwick |
| Dec-Feb | Mangoes | Ayr | Ayr |

| Harvest period | Crop | Area | Nearest Agency |
|---|---|---|---|
| *South Australia* | | | |
| Feb-Mar | Wine grapes | Southern Vales | Noarlunga |
| Feb-Mar | Dried fruits | Riverland | Berri |
| Feb-Mar | Apples,pears | Adelaide Hills | Payneham |
| Feb-Apr | Wine grapes | Riverland | Berri |
| Feb-Apr | Peaches | Riverland | Berri |
| Feb-Apr | Wine grapes | Barossa Valley | Gawler |
| Jun-Aug | Navel oranges | Riverland | Berri |
| Jun-Sep | Pruning | Riverland | Berri |
| Sep-Jan | Oranges (Juicing and packing) | Riverland | Berri |
| Oct-Feb | Strawberries | Adelaide Hills | Payneham |
| Dec-Feb | Apricots | Riverland | Berri |
| *Tasmania* | | | |
| Feb-May | Potatoes | Scottsdale | Mowbray |
| Jan-Mar | Strawberries | Ringarooma | Mowbray |
| Mar-Apr | Hops | Scottsdale Derwent Valley Devonport | Mowbray Glenorchy Devonport |
| Mar-Apr | Grapes | Pipers River Tamar Valley | Mowbray Mowbray |
| Feb-Apr | Grapes | Berridale | Glenorchy |
| Mar-Apr | Pears, apples | Huon Valley | Huonville |
| Feb-May | Apples | Eastern Shore Bicheno Tasman Peninsula | Eastern Eastern |
| Dec-Jan | Raspberries | Elizabeth Town Derwent Valley Devonport | Launceston Glenorchy Devonport |

| Harvest period | Crop | Area | Nearest Agency |
|---|---|---|---|
| Jun-Aug | Brassica | Devonport | Devonport |

*Western Australia*

| Harvest period | Crop | Area | Nearest Agency |
|---|---|---|---|
| Feb-Mar | Wildflowers | Coorow | Geraldton |
| Feb-Apr | Grapes | Albany | Albany |
| | | Mt Barker | Albany |
| | | Swan Valley | Midland |
| Feb-May | Apples | Manjimup | Manjimup |
| | | Pemberton | |
| | | Bridgetown | |
| | | Donnybrooke | Bunbury |
| Mar-Jun | Rock lobster | Geraldton | Geraldton |
| Mar-Jun | Oats, wheat barley | Merredin | Merredin |
| | | Northam | Northam |
| Mar-Oct | Prawning, scalloping | Carnarvon | Carnarvon |
| Apr-Jun | Oats, wheat barley | Wagin | Collie |
| | | Gnowangerup | Gnowangerup |
| | | Katanning | Katanning |
| | | Williams | Collie |
| | | Narrogin | Collie |
| | | West Arthur | Collie |
| | | Geraldton | Geraldton |
| Apr-Jun | Oats, wheat | Bindoon | Midland |
| | | Lower Chittering | |
| Apr-Jun | Oats, wheat | Moora | Midland |
| Apr-Nov | Watermelons | Coorow | Geraldton |
| May-Jun | Oats, wheat | Salmon Gums | Esperance |
| May-Sep | Zucchini, squash, watermelons rockmelon | Kununurra | Kununurra |
| Jul-Dec | Wildflowers | Coorow | Geraldton |

| Harvest period | Crop | Area | Nearest Agency |
|---|---|---|---|
| Sep-Nov | Mangoes | Kununurra | Kununurra |
| Oct-Dec | Oats, wheat, barley | Merredin | Merredin |
| Jun-Dec | Tomatoes | Carnavon | Carnavon |
| Aug-Nov | Wildflowers | Machea | Midland |
| Oct-Jan | Oats, wheat, barley | Geraldton | Geraldton |
| Nov-Dec | Oats, wheat, barley | Albany | Albany |
| 15th Nov-30th Jun | Rock lobster | Fremantle<br>Dongara<br>Kalbarri<br>Mandurah<br>Jurien Bay<br>Geraldton | Fremantle<br>Fremantle<br>Fremantle<br>Mandurah<br>Geraldton<br>Geraldton |
| Nov-Dec | Wheat, barley | Moora<br>Northam<br>Esperance | Midland<br>Northam<br>Esperance |
| All year bananas | | Kununurra | Kununurra |

## Pay and conditions for fruit pickers

The amount you earn from fruit picking will vary depending on your speed and the crop you are picking. In the majority of cases you will be paid according to your output. Some crops are more profitable than others — grapes are considered to be one of the most profitable crops because they are relatively easy to get to and pick. Even a novice grape-picker could expect to earn at least $A350 a week. At the other end of the scale are the likes of apples and oranges. These are notoriously unprofitable for the beginner because you have to keep going up and down a ladder to get the fruit. Placing the ladder is considered to be an art in itself.

Conditions can vary as much as pay but do not expect any five-star treatment, as one grape-picker in Mildura explained, 'When I reached the farm I was confronted by a corrugated-iron shed which I thought was the tractor shed. In fact, it turned out to be the staff accommodation. For the first few days I had to sleep on the concrete floor, but then I was afforded the "luxury" of having a rusty bedstead on which to lay my sleeping bag. To be honest I was lucky to have any type of free accommodation because most unexperienced pickers have to provide their own tent.

'We usually ate together in a fly-infested kitchen and after the first week we gave up cooking altogether and lived off hamburgers and, of course, grapes. Most of the growers in the area were tough men who always tried to get away with whatever they could. In the end three of us got fed up with our boss's behaviour and walked out. We ended up sitting on the pavement on the main street and after five minutes we had another offer of employment. Fruit picking tends to take you into cowboy country but it is well worth the experience.'

As well as taking your own accommodation it is also helpful, if not essential at times, to have your own transport too. Check with the Centrelink first to find out the local conditions.

## HOSPITALITY WORK

This is one area in which people on holiday working visas have traditionally found a variety of casual work. Whether it is as a potwasher (dishwasher) in a five-star hotel or a barman at the tourist resort at Ayers Rock, catering staff are in demand in all areas of the Australian hospitality industry.

Although experience is not always necessary for this type of work it does pay to look clean, tidy and respectable when applying for jobs. If you do have experience as a barperson, a chef or a waiter/waitress then take references with you to convince employers of your suitability. Lots of other people will be looking for the same types of jobs as yourself, so you will need a certain amount of luck and, at times, determination to land a job in hospitality. Check local newspapers and the Centrelink; if there are no suitable vacancies then put on your glad rags and your best smile and go knocking on some doors. It is conceivable that you could spend several days without success but do not become down-hearted. Keep trying and do not be afraid to go to the same place two, three or four times — workers are frequently leaving or being fired from bars and restaurants and if you arrive at one of these moments then you could be in luck.

One of the things that is beginning to count against holiday working visa holders is that some of their predecessors have only spent a week, or even a couple of days, in a particular job before moving on. Although there is no reason why they should not do this it does not endear casual workers to a lot of employers. This is most apparent in tourist areas such as the Queensland island resorts and Cairns. As one nightclub manager explained, 'About two years ago most of my staff were travellers on holiday working visas and it can get extremely tiring if they work for a fortnight and then leave. There is never a problem in replacing them but the paperwork involved in putting on new staff can be considerable. My advice to people who know they will only be in an area for a short period of time is to avoid employment — you will only ruin it for people who come after you.' How you convince employers that you will turn up for work for a longer period of time is up to individuals but it is best not to lie.

Another factor counting against casual workers is the current recession and a downturn in the Australian tourist industry. This has led to more native Australians chasing fewer openings and there have been some cases of travellers being unable to find this type of casual work in certain areas.

In order to try and maximise your chances of employment in the hospitality industry you should:

● Look at it as a serious option, not a continuous party for which you expect to be paid.

● Be well prepared — if you have had relevant experience then take documents to show this. If you have no experience try and get some before you go.

● Be prepared to do any job, even if it is cleaning fish-heads or peeling mountains of potatoes.

● Make sure you are neat and tidy.

● If possible, take black trousers, black shoes and a white shirt/blouse with you.

● Be determined in your job-hunting — there are hospitality jobs to be had, they are just a bit harder to track down at present.
● Be prepared to convince employers that you will be around for more than a couple of days.

## OTHER JOB POSSIBILITIES

### Factory work
If you have a high boredom threshold then you could consider working in a factory packing anything from pineapples to soap. A good source of information about job availability is fellow travellers who have 'been there and done it', as they say. It is also worth following the fruit picking cycle — a lot of this produce will be packed for consumption in

other parts of the country or overseas. The pay tends to be good for this type of work but you may be driven crazy if you do it for too long.

## Fishing

There are some jobs to be had on prawn fishing vessels out of Broome, Darwin, Cairns and Townsville. The main jobs for men are net-mending and prawn-sorting, while women are usually taken on board as cooks. A set of good sea-legs and willingness to work hard are the best qualifications for this type of work but it is worth remembering that you may be at sea for several weeks at one time. Payment is in the form of a fixed wage or a share of the catch. Since the number of prawns being caught is smaller than it used to be a more stable option is to take the former. If you are a female member of crew you should make it perfectly clear what your role on board is going to include — and, more importantly, what it will not include. You can look for this type of work through the Centrelink, or approach privately-owned boats or large companies, although these will probably tell you that you have to be a member of a seamans unions.

## Jackaroo/Jillaroo

For people with farm experience of some description it may be possible to get a job as a jackaroo or a jillaroo (a sheep station assistant). Although it sounds romantic the chances are that you will not be riding across the outback on your trusty steed. In reality there can be a lot of sitting around on a sheep station — if not you will be doing all the jobs that no-one else can be bothered with. Ask someone who has done it before you commit yourself.

## Labouring

This area of employment was hit harder than most as a result of the recession and is still trying to recover. As the building trade contracts so the need for labourers dwindles. You could try visiting building sites to see if there is any work going but the best bet is to go to a relevant Centrelink *early* in the morning. If there is any need for labourers they will be picked from the pool of men who gather at or before 6am. This is done on a day to day basis but it could lead to some useful contacts.

## Mining

The more robust and adventurous could try and find work in the mining areas of north Western Australia or the Northern Territory. Due to recent contraction in the industry there are few jobs advertised in the local newspapers or Centrelink so it is a case of going to the mines themselves. Since they can be hundreds of miles from any major city this is quite a risk if you do not find a job. On the other hand you will have a memorable experience getting there and back. Another possibility is the gold mining town of Kalgoorlie in Western Australia or Charters Towers in Queensland. If you are feeling particularly dedicated you could go looking for gold yourself, as one traveller, Andy Schmitke, did in the hills near Townsville in northern Queensland: 'I bought a second-hand gold dredger (approximately $A800) and four of us headed for the hills in best goldrush tradition. The work consisted of finding a suitable looking stream and then using the dredger to sift through the mud. We did it for eight weeks and although we did not make a fortune we did earn a few hundred dollars, and got a real buzz from the pioneering feeling.'

## Miscellaneous opportunities
Travellers in Australia have been known to get jobs drinking beer in commercials or singing cockney songs in an 'English' pub. Keep an open mind about job opportunities and not just in terms of the type of job you would do at home. It may even be worthwhile brushing up on a few choruses of 'Knees up, Mother Brown'!

Although casual employment is an important part of a working holiday in Australia it should be looked upon as a benefit rather than a necessity. Make sure you take enough money to support you for a reasonable length of time during your visit. If you arrive with only a few dollars in your pocket, hoping to find work immediately, then you may quickly find yourself in a miserable situation if you cannot find a job. There is still plenty of work available for holiday working visa holders but it should be approached in the same way as looking for a permanent job somewhere.

## CHECKLIST

1.   Be aware of the current economic situation in Australia.

2.   Be prepared to work at getting work — do not consider it as your right.

3.   Use the Centrelink to find out about the availability of jobs in various areas.

4.   Be willing to promote yourself and use your initiative.

5.  Take with you any documents which could help your job-hunting.

6.  Ask your fellow travellers about their experiences of working and looking for work in Australia.

7.  Do not be easily put off if you initially find it difficult to find a job.

8.  Make sure you have finances to support you during your first few months in Australia.

9.  Be prepared to accept Australian work ethics.

10. Make the most of your time working — if you are not enjoying it then move on.

# 13

## Relocation

Relocation for any job is a difficult business even if it is in your own country. However, if your relocation is international then the problems tend to multiply. Due to the complex nature of moving yourself, your family and all your possessions to Australia there are a number of companies who specialise in all aspects of removal and also personal travel.

### REMOVAL

Unless you want to ship a Chieftain tank you can transport virtually anything to Australia. This includes:

- cars;
- motorbikes;
- animals;
- boats;
- complete household goods;
- excess baggage;
- miscellaneous items.

There are a number of firms who specialise in shipping goods to Australia and it is worth using their experience. A few points should be considered when choosing a company and organising your removal:

1. Shipping costs are usually calculated on volume and so you will have to give your removal firm precise details of the items you need moved, or the sizes of trunks, cartons and tea-chests which you plan to use.

2. If you are planning on a substantial shipment it is advisable to get estimates from various companies before you commit yourself.

3.  You must tell the removal company your final destination in Australia because this could effect the overall cost. For instance, if you plan on settling in a port city such as Perth or Sydney then the cost of moving the goods from the port to your home will be small. On the other hand, if you are going to be living in Alice Springs then the extra transport cost will be considerable: charges are based on mileage from the port of entry.

4.  Check varying prices and conditions of service from at least four different companies.

5.  It is worth making initial enquiries over the phone but make sure you have precise information about what you want.

6.  Do not ask for a quote too far ahead of your time of departure (over six months) because prices will invariably have increased by then.

7.  Alternatively do not leave things too late — remember, it will take your goods up to three months to arrive in Australia.

8.  As well as the charge by the removal firm there may be additional costs in the form of storage, quarantine (for any animals shipped), demurrage and Customs duty.

## Removal companies

*General*

Abels International, 4a North Orbital, Napsbury Lane, St. Albans, Herts AL1 1XB. Tel: 01727 837417.

All Route Shipping (NI) Ltd, 14-16 West Bank Road, Belfast Harbour Estate, Belfast BT3 9JL. Tel: 01232 370223.

Anglo Pacific International Plc, Unit 1 Bush Industrial Estate, Standard Road, North Acton, London NW10 6DF. Tel: 0800 328 2382.

Avalon. Tel: London 0208 451 6336; Manchester 0161 945 9685; Scotland 01324 634170.

Bishop Blatchpack, Kestrel Way, Sowton Industrial Estate, Exeter, Devon EX2 7PA. Tel: 01392 420404.

Copsey & Company Ltd, Danes Road, Romford, Essex, London RM7 0HL. Tel: 0800 289 658.

Crown Worldwide Movers/Scotpac International Movers, Gartsherrie Road, Coatbridge, Glasgow. Tel: 0141 776 7191.

Davies Turner, Worldwide Movers, Overseas House, Stewarts Road, London SW8 4UG. Tel: 0208 682 2020.

Doree-Bonner, 0800 289541 (Enquiries and quotations).

Double E Overseas Removals Ltd, Movements House, Ajax Works, Hertford Road, Barking, Essex IG11 8BW. Tel: 0208 591 6929.

Econopak Removals Limited, Unit K, Abbey Wharf Industrial Estate, Kingsbridge Road, Barking, Essex IG11 0BT. Tel: 0208 591 3434.

Harrison, Lennon and Hoy, Rochester Way, Dartford, Kent DA1 3QY. Tel: 01322 555757.

Hoults Removals. Tel: North London 0208 367 7600; Northwest London 0208 2198150; Birmingham 0121 359 7541; Manchester 0161 865 0071; Edinburgh 0131 225 6764; Glasgow 0141 336 3335.

John Mason International Ltd, 2 Mill Lane Industrial Estate, Mill Lane, Croydon, Surrey CR0 4AA. Tel: 0208 667 1133.

McConnell Removals Limited, Unit 11 Mullusk Park, Newtownabbey, Northern Ireland. Tel: 01232 843631.

Personal Shipping Services, 8 Redcross Way, London Bridge, London SE1 9HR. Tel: 0800 614508.

Pickfords, 492 Great Cambridge Road, Enfield, Middlesex EN1 3SA. Tel: 0208 219 8200 (Head Office)/ 0800 28 92 29 (Enquiries).

*Animal freight specialists*

Golden Arrow Shippers, Lydbury North, Shropshire SY7 8AY. Tel: 015888 240 and 606.

Ladyhaye Livestock Shipping, Hare Lane, Blindley Heath, Lingfield, Surrey RH7 6JB. Tel: 01342 832161.

Par Air Livestock Shipping Services, Stanway, Colchester, Essex. Tel: 01206 330332.

Pinehawk Livestock Shippers, Church Road, Carlton, Newmarket, Suffolk CB8 9LA. Tel: 01223 290249.

Skymaster Air Cargo Ltd, Room 15, Building 305, Cargo Centre, Manchester Airport, Altrincham, Cheshire WA15 8UX. Tel: 0161 436 2190.

Transpet, 24 Somerton Rd, London NW2 1SA. Tel 0207 586 1231..

Whitelea Skydogs, Cross Green, Matlock, Derbys DE4 2JT. Tel: 01629 734000.

Since overseas removal companies can go bust just as easily as anyone else it is advisable to choose a company which is a member of **The Association of International Removers** (AIR). This not only means that the company has been carefully vetted and specialises in international removal but also that it is covered by the AIR Customer Payment Guarantee. This protects your full payment and in the event of a company ceasing trading AIR will take over responsibility for management of your removal.

## TRAVEL ARRANGEMENTS

Once you have arranged for your goods and possessions to be transported to Australia it is time to think about getting yourself the 10,000 miles to the other side of the world. The main considerations when doing this are:

- cost;
- comfort;
- speed.

Cost will probably be the most important factor for most people but until you have spent forty hours and numerous transit stops in getting to Australia you do not know the real meaning of jet-lag. When booking a flight of this nature it pays to deal with travel agents who specialise in long haul travel. Not only will they be able to offer you the best deal (hopefully), they will also be able to give you some hints and tips from their own experiences. Some of the companies who have a good reputation for helping people get to Australia as quickly, cheaply and as comfortably as possible are:

- Anglo Pacific, 135 Earls Court Road, London SW5 9RH. Tel: 0800 328 2382.

- Australian Air Fare Centre, 102 New Street, Birmingham B2 4HQ. Tel: 0121 633 3232. Special services for migrant travellers, including 40kg baggage allowance and 50 per cent child discount.

- Austravel, 50 Conduit Street, London W1. Tel: 0207 734 7755.

- Bridge The World Travel Centre, 4 Regent Place, London W1R 5FB Tel: 0207 734 7447

- STA Travel, 86 Old Brompton Road, London SW7; 117 Euston Road, London NW1; 75 Deansgate, Manchester; 25 Queens Road, Bristol; 88 Vicar Lane, Leeds; 19 High Street, Oxford; 38 Sidney

Street, Cambridge. For information about flights to Australia —
Tel: 0207 361 6161.

● Taprobane Travel, 4 Kingly Street, London W1R 5LF. Tel: 0207
437 6272/3.

● Trailfinders, 42-50 Earls Court Road, London W8 6EJ. Tel: 0207
938 3366. 215 Kensington High Street, London W8 7RG. Tel: 020
7937 5400.


## ACCOMMODATION

Short-term accommodation can be one of the biggest worries for people arriving in Australia, particularly if they are migrating and they
have not arranged to buy property yet, or do not have family with
whom to stay.

As a sample these are some of the rates you can expect to pay for various types of accommodation in different Australian cities. These rates are
generally for people looking for accommodation from one to four weeks.

### Sydney
*Studio* From $A350 per week (two people).
*One bedroom, self-contained units* From $A400 per week (two people).
*Two to three bedroom, self-contained units* From $A550 per week (two
people).
*Hotel/motel units* From $A425 per week (double).
*Note* Rates are more expensive for accommodation which is near to the
city centre or beach holiday areas.

### Brisbane
*One bedroom apartments* From $A320 per week.
*Two to three bedroom apartments* From $A400 per week (two persons).
*Four bedroom apartments (Limited supply)* From $A575 per week.
*Note* Since Brisbane is Australia's holiday state a large part of the year
is classified as peak — the more notice you give the better chance you
have of being offered a lower rate.

### Perth
*One bedroom apartment* From $A275 per week.
*Two to three bedroom apartments* From $A350 per week.
*Hotel/motel units* From $A360 per week (double).

## Melbourne
*One bedroom apartment* From $A250 per week.
*Two to three bedroom apartments* From $A360 per week.
*Hotel/motel units* $A390 per week.

## Adelaide
*One bedroom apartments* From $A270 per week.
*Two to three bedroom apartments* From $A320 per week.
*Hotel/motel units* From $A440 per week.

## Other contacts for accommodation
The magazine *Australian Outlook* offers an accommodation service for most areas of Australia, for which they charge a £15 fee. For further information contact: Consyl Publishing, 3 Buckhurst Road, Bexhill-on-Sea, East Sussex TN40 1QF. Tel: 01424 223111.

## SETTLING IN

Although it will not be as obvious as in some other countries, you will experience culture-shock when you first arrive in Australia: the climate, the politics, the way people talk, general attitudes, the media, the food, the culture and a hundred and one other areas that may seem similar to those at home but which have numerous subtle differences. For instance, Australians speak English but they also have one of the most colourful and expressive colloquial vocabularies in the world.

The best way to come to terms with your new environment is to become absorbed in it slowly rather than to try and change into a 'true-blue' Aussie overnight. Take time to look around you to see how people act and what type of behaviour is acceptable and unacceptable. Watch a variety of television programmes and read newspapers to find out what is going on in the country and what makes it tick. But most of all, talk to people. This is the best way to learn things and it will pay to be an interested observer initially. Avoid being opinionated or over-bearing — you are the new kid on the block and you should try and make a good impression. If you do, it will stand you in good stead for the future.

It may take several months, or even a few years, before you feel properly settled in your new surroundings but it is something that should be done gradually and persevered with.

# Glossary of Employment Terms

**Accord** This is the agreement reached between the Federal Government and the Australian Council of Trade Unions in 1983. Its main aim is to offer tax trade-offs in return for moderate wage increases. It was instigated by Bob Hawke and its future is now uncertain.

**ACTU** Australian Council of Trade Unions. The equivalent of the British TUC.

**A/H** After hours. Used by many tradespeople who can be contacted for jobs after normal working hours.

**Annual leave** This is generally a minimum of four weeks paid leave a year. See also **Leave loading**.

**Assets test** A means test on pensioners which can reduce their pensions in line with their assets.

**Award rate** This is the minimum rate of pay which can be offered to employees. Each profession has a different award rate which also deals with conditions of employment as well as pay.

**Bludger** Someone who avoids work at every opportunity.

**Centrelink** (CES) This is the major feature in the public sector recruitment network. It has offices throughout the country and offers advice as well as advertising the current job vacancies.

**Compo** Workers compensation. A popular concept among Australian workers; even the smallest injury will be put under the compo spotlight.

**Dobber** Anyone who tells tales on their fellow workmates. In a society which prides itself on workers' solidarity dobbing is looked upon as a cardinal sin and anyone who is accused of this is likely to be sent to Coventry, or perhaps Sydney.

**Dragging the chain** Someone who does not do their fair share of the work — something that may be done by a **bludger**.

**Equal Employment Opportunity** (EEO) A Commonwealth Government policy to discourage discrimination in employment. Employers following this policy consider job applicants on their ability and regardless of sex, race, marital status and other such factors.

163

**Flat-out-like-a-lizard-drinking** Someone working their socks off.

**Flexitime** An arrangement where workers can start and leave work at earlier or later times to normal. Debits or credits of working hours can be built up within specified limits enabling a 'flex day' to be taken off on occasions. Flexitime conditions vary from company to company and depend on the relevant award for that industry. Flexitime is most common in the public service.

**Full-time employment** Any job where you work more than 30 hours a week.

**Group certificate** A yearly statement of earnings issued by the employer and used by the employee to prepare the dreaded tax return.

**Gun** The best, and fastest, worker. Frequently applied in industries such as fruit-picking or anything where you have to produce a certain amount a day.

**Hard yakka** Hard work — definitely not done by a **bludger**.

**Job sharing** As employment rises, more and more people are embracing the concept of job sharing, whereby two or more people share the duties and responsibilities of one job. The hours and conditions are arranged to suit the employees.

**Leave loading** This is a particularly Australian concept which allows for an extra 17.5 per cent to be added to workers' annual holiday pay. An extremely civilised arrangement.

**Long service leave** Three months paid leave usually granted after either 10 or 15 years of continuous employment with one firm.

**Medicare** The system of national health care. Provides for free hospital treatment and 85 per cent of general practitioners' fees. A tax of 1.7 per cent is levied on all wage earners in order to finance Medicare.

**O** A suffix used with a variety of occupations, such as journo, milko, garbo (garbage collector), muso, and so on.

**Offsider** An assistant.

**Overtime** Any hours worked in excess of regular full-time hours. Overtime rates are usually at time-and-a-half or double-time.

**Part-time work** (also called **casual employment**) Any job where you work less than 30 hours a week. You do not always have the same rights as full-time workers but awards for part-time work usually contain sufficient provisions to protect workers.

**Penalty rates** Due to the **accord** and **award** agreements, workers are paid at higher rates if they work at weekends, at night or on shift work. Workers are often happy to work at unsociable hours because of penalty rates.

**Piece work** Work where you are paid on how much you produce.

**Severance pay** Compensation paid by a firm to an employee whose services are no longer required because of technological changes or other factors.

**Shift work** Most shift work is divided into three sections — day, afternoon, and night shift. All shifts are usually eligible for **penalty rates** but night shift attracts the highest rate.

**Sickie** An unscheduled day off when you do not feel like going to work because of a hangover, the sun is shining or you just do not feel like working. An increasing problem in the Australian workforce, since some workers believe that it is their right to take a certain number of sickies a year.

**Sick leave** Paid leave when you are suffering from the sickie malaise. It also applies when you are genuinely sick although there is a limit to how many sick days you can have a year.

**Smoko** A tea break — some industries would be brought to a halt if its workers were not allowed their smoko. Smoking is not obligatory.

**Special leave** This is extra leave which is granted in exceptional circumstances, such as the death of a close relative, attendance at jury service, or private study.

**Superannuation** A scheme financed by either employers, or employers and employees, which assures the employee an income after retirement.

**TAFE: Technical and Further Education** colleges. This is the main vocational education body in Australia. It covers a wide range of professions and has a large number of colleges in all states.

**Tax agent** Someone to fill in your tax form. Although they charge a fee it is usually well worth it, not only for the time they can save you but also because of the refund which they may be able to calculate.

**TFN: Tax File Number** A number which you must have if you intend to work in Australia. It can be obtained by filling in a form from any tax office in Australia.

# Useful Addresses

Australian Bureau of Statistics, PO Box 10, Belconnen, ACT 2616. Tel: 06 252 6112.

Australian High Commission, Australia House, Strand, London WC2B 4LA. Tel: 0207 379 4334.

Australian Department of Employment, Workplace Relations and Small Business, PO Box 9880, Canberra, ACT 2601. Tel: 06 837008.

Department of Industrial Relations, GPO Box 9879, Canberra, ACT 2601. Tel: 06 243 7333.

Department of Immigration, Local Government and Ethnic Affairs, Central Office, Benjamin Offices, Chan Street, Belconnen, ACT 2617. Tel: 06 574111.

Department of Family and Community Services, Australia House, Strand, London WC2B 4LA.

Department of Family and Community Services, Juliana House, Bowes Street, Philip, ACT 2606. Tel: 06 891444.

Department of Trade, Edmund Barton Building, Kings Avenue, Barton, ACT 2600. Tel: 062 723911.

Financial and Migrant Information Service, Commonwealth Bank of Australia, 1 Kingsway, London WC2. Tel: 0207 379 0955.

National Office of Overseas Skills Recognition (NOOSR), GPO Box 1407, Canberra City, ACT. Tel: 06 276 7636.

## Trade

Agent-General for New South Wales, New South Wales House, 66 Strand, London WC2N 5LZ. Tel: 0207 839 6651.

Agent-General for Victoria, Victoria House, Melbourne Place, Strand, London WC2B 4LG. Tel: 0207 836 2656.

Agent-General for Queensland, Queensland House, 392-393 Strand, London WC2R 0LZ. Tel: 0207 836 1333.

Agent-General for Western Australia, Western Australia House, 115-116 Strand, London WC2R 0AJ. Tel: 0207 240 2881.

Australian Trade Commission (AUSTRADE), Australia House, Strand, London WC2B 4LA. Tel: 0207 887 5326.

## WEB ADDRESSES

### Government sites
Federal Government: www.fed.gov.au/
London High Commission: www.australia.org.uk/
Centrelink: www.centrelink.gov.au/
Tax office: www.ato.gov.au/
Department of Employment, Workplace Relations and Small Business: www.dewrsb.gov.au/
Department of Family and Community Services: www.dss.gov.au/
Department of Education, Training and Youth Affairs: www.detya.gov.au/
Treasury Web services: www. treasury. gov.au/
Department of Health and Age Concern: www. health. gov.au/
Australian Institute of Health and Welfare: www.aihw.gov.au/
Bureau of Statistics: www.abs.gov.au/
Australian Workplace: www.workplace.gov.au

### Employment
JobSearch: www.jobsearch.gov.au/
Job Network: www.jobnetwork.gov.au/
WageNet: www.wagenet.gov.au/
Web Wombat Employment: www.webwombat.com.au/jobs/
Yellow Pages: www.yellowpages.cpm.au/ (Enter 'Employment' or 'Employment Agencies' in the search facility)

### General
Fact sheets about Australia: www.dfat.gov.au/factslfssalphaindex.html
National Library of Australia: www.nia.gov.au/
Australia's Cultural Network: www.can.net.au/
Newspapers (all newspaper websites): www.nia.gov.au/oz/npapers.html
Sydney Morning Herald: www.smh.com.au/
The Age: www.theage.com.au/
The Australian: www. news. com.au/
Tourism: www.aussie.net.au/

# Further Reading

## MAGAZINES AND NEWSPAPERS

*Australian News,* Outbound Newspapers Limited, 1 Commercial Road, Eastbourne, East Sussex BN21 3XQ. Tel: 01323 412001.

*Australian Outlook,* 1 Buckhurst Road, Town Hall Square, Bexhill-on-Sea, East Sussex TN40 1QF. Tel: 01424 223111.

*Brisbane Courier-Mail,* Campbell Street, Bowen Hills, Brisbane.

*The Adelaide Advertiser,* 121 King William Street, Adelaide.

*The Melbourne Age,* 250 Spencer Street, Melbourne.

*The Sydney Morning Herald,* 235 Jones Street, Broadway, NSW 2007.

*The West Australian,* 219 St. George's Terrace, Perth 6000.

## BOOKS

*Australian Careers Guide,* David Royce Publishing, 44 Regent Street, Redfern, NSW.

*Living & Working in Australia* by Laura Veltman, How To Books.

*Getting a Job Abroad* by Roger Jones, How To Book.

*Planning Your Gap Year* by Nick Vandome, How To Books.

*Cost of Living and Housing Survey*, Commonwealth Bank of Australia.

*Telecom National Business Directory,* Telecom Australia (available from most large libraries).

*Jobsons Year Book of Public Companies,* Dun and Bradstreet (Publications), 24 Albert Street, South Melbourne, Victoria 3205.

*Smart Start,* Hobsons Press (Australia), 270 Pitt Street, Sydney, NSW 2000.

*What Job Suits You?,* Hobsons Press (Australia), 270 Pitt Street, Sydney, NSW 2000.

*Job Prospects — Australia,* Hobsons Press (Australia), 270 Pitt Street, Sydney, NSW 2000.

*What Jobs Pay,* Hobsons Press (Australia), 270 Pitt Street, Sydney, NSW 2000.

*The Job Book — Life After School,* Hobsons Press (Australia), 270 Pitt Street, Sydney, NSW 2000.

*Business Destination Australia/New Zealand,* Business Migration Program, Australian Consulates, Embassies and Commissions.

# Index